CAMBRIDGE LIBRARY COLLECTION

Books of enduring scholarly value

Travel, Middle East and Asia Minor

This collection of travel narratives, primarily from the nineteenth century, describing the topography, antiquities and inhabitants of the Middle East, from Turkey, Kurdistan and Persia to Mesopotamia, Syria, Jerusalem, Sinai, Egypt and Arabia. While some travellers came to study Christian sites and manuscripts, others were fascinated by Islamic culture and still others by the remains of ancient civilizations. Among the authors are several daring female explorers.

Ludolph von Suchem's Description of the Holy Land, and of the Way Thither

Beyond the fact that he made a journey to the Holy Land between 1336 and 1341, very little is known about Ludolf von Suchem (whose first name may in fact have been Rudolf). However, his work has long been regarded as a major source of information about the eastern Mediterranean in the fourteenth century, owing to its high level of detail. Ludolf states his intention to describe the region, its buildings, towns, fortified places, people, customs, stories and legends, drawing on both his own observations, and on information from the 'kings, princes, nobles and lords' with whom he spent days and nights in conversation. Some stories are clearly travellers' tales, but others, like his account of the fall of Acre (1291), based on reports by eyewitnesses, are both full and convincing. This English translation, by Aubrey Stewart (1844–1918), of Ludolf's Latin text (also reissued in the Cambridge Library Collection) was published in 1895.

Cambridge University Press has long been a pioneer in the reissuing of out-of-print titles from its own backlist, producing digital reprints of books that are still sought after by scholars and students but could not be reprinted economically using traditional technology. The Cambridge Library Collection extends this activity to a wider range of books which are still of importance to researchers and professionals, either for the source material they contain, or as landmarks in the history of their academic discipline.

Drawing from the world-renowned collections in the Cambridge University Library and other partner libraries, and guided by the advice of experts in each subject area, Cambridge University Press is using state-of-the-art scanning machines in its own Printing House to capture the content of each book selected for inclusion. The files are processed to give a consistently clear, crisp image, and the books finished to the high quality standard for which the Press is recognised around the world. The latest print-on-demand technology ensures that the books will remain available indefinitely, and that orders for single or multiple copies can quickly be supplied.

The Cambridge Library Collection brings back to life books of enduring scholarly value (including out-of-copyright works originally issued by other publishers) across a wide range of disciplines in the humanities and social sciences and in science and technology.

Ludolph von Suchem's Description of the Holy Land, and of the Way Thither

Written in the Year A.D. 1350

Edited and translated by
Aubrey Stewart

CAMBRIDGE
UNIVERSITY PRESS

University Printing House, Cambridge, CB2 8BS, United Kingdom

Published in the United States of America by Cambridge University Press, New York

Cambridge University Press is part of the University of Cambridge.
It furthers the University's mission by disseminating knowledge in the pursuit of
education, learning and research at the highest international levels of excellence.

www.cambridge.org
Information on this title: www.cambridge.org/9781108061827

© in this compilation Cambridge University Press 2013

This edition first published 1895
This digitally printed version 2013

ISBN 978-1-108-06182-7 Paperback

Palestine Pilgrims' Text Society.

LUDOLPH VON SUCHEM'S
Description of the Holy Land,

AND OF THE WAY THITHER.

WRITTEN IN THE YEAR
A.D. 1350.

Translated

BY

A U B R E Y   S T E W A R T ,   M.A.

LONDON:
24, HANOVER SQUARE, W.
1895.

PREFACE TO LUDOLPHUS DE SUCHEM.

NOTHING seems to be known about Ludolph beyond what can be gathered from his book. In the dedication he tells us that he was the rector of the parish church of Suchem, in the diocese of Paderborn. Where Suchem was, and whether it should be spelled Sudheim, is what Dr. F. Deycks declares to be a *Räthsel*. Dr. Deycks, professor at the Royal Academy at Munster, edited Ludolph in 1851 for the Stuttgart *Litterarische Verein*, and it is his edition that I have followed in my translation. Furthermore, Ludolph speaks of Baldwin von Steinfurt, Bishop of Paderborn, who held the see from 1340 to 1361, as his gracious lord. In the colophon he says that he wrote his book out of the devotion and respect which he owed to him. Perhaps Bishop Baldwin helped him to write it, and perhaps he was one of the noble lords with whom he associated during his five years' sojourn in the Holy Land. He·was there from 1336 to 1341 ; he did not, as some have imagined, return thither in 1350. Ludolph returned home in 1341, and twice was in great danger at sea. Near the end of his book he alludes to the ' Jew-baiting ' in Germany, 1348-49, as a new event, which agrees well with his book having been written in the year 1350.

As we know so little of Ludolph from his own writings, the next step obviously is to consult those of Wilhelm von Boldinsel,[1] to whom he alludes as a fellow-traveller in the Holy Land. Wilhelm von Boldinsel (a name, by the way, to which he was only entitled through his mother) seems to have begun as a Dominican monk, but afterwards to have led a wandering life under the protection of that Cardinal Talleyrand Périgord who strove so ineffectually to avert bloodshed before the battle of Poictiers. Wilhelm was sent to the Holy Land on some sort of diplomatic mission, accompanied by an armed escort. He wrote an account of his pilgrimage—for he visited the holy places— in the year 1336.[2] Ludolph has copied many entire sentences from Boldinsel, and in many passages their descriptions tally, but one does not learn much that is new about the Holy Land from Boldinsel, and one learns nothing about Ludolph.

Another contemporary writer is John of Hildesheim. All that is known of this favourite mediaeval author may be found in Trithemius's *Liber de scriptoribus ecclesiasticis*, tom. cxvii.; in Oudinus's *Commentarium de scriptoribus eccl. antiquis*, iii., p. 1275; in Fabricius's *Bibliotheca med. et inf. Latin*, iv. 8; and especially in *Bibliotheca Carmelitana, Aurelianis*, 1752, ii. p. 4. He is called a Saxon, or a Westphalian, and probably was born at

---

[1] See 'Die Edelherren von Boldensele oder Boldensen. 1. Zur Genealogie der Geschlechts; 2. Des Edelherrn Wilhelm von Bodensele Reise nach den Gelobten Land. Von Archiv. Secretair Dr. C. L. Grotefend. Hannover, 1855, Hofbuchdruckerei der Gebr. Janecke.'

[2] T. Wright, in his 'Introduction' to 'Early Travels in Palestine' (Bohn, 1848), has a mistake about Boldinsel's date. He landed at Tyre in 1332, and was at Jerusalem in 1333.

Hildesheim. He became a Carmelite Friar, studied at Avignon, whither he went with Petrus Thomas, general of his order, under Clement VI. (Peter Roger, Archbishop of Rouen, Pope 1342-52), and became Doctor of Divinity and professor. In 1358 he was appointed *biblicus* at Paris by the chapter held at Bordeaux. Afterwards he returned to Germany and became Prior of Cassel ; as such, he was sent on a mission to Rome in 1360. On his return he was made prior of the convent of Marienau, mediated the peace between the Bishop of Hildesheim and the Duke of Brunswick, and died in his convent in 1375, where he lies buried in the choir, beside the founder of the convent, Count Gleichen. He wrote many works : *Chronica Historiarum, De monstris in ecclesia, De Antichristo, In turpia pingentem, Defensorium sui ordinis, De fonte Vitae, Contra Judaeos sermones, Epistolae, et quaedam alia.* His *Historia trium Regum* had an immense and immediate success. It is dedicated to Florence de Weuelkoven, Bishop of Munster, in Westphalia, who held that see from 1364 to 1379, and died 1393 as Bishop of Utrecht. As the author died in 1375, his book must have been written between 1364 and 1375. Some dates mentioned in his *Historia* point to this period ; he alludes to events which took place in the years 1340, 1341, and 1361.

I have extracted these details concerning John of Hildesheim from C. Horstmann's edition of the *Historia trium Regum*, because I wished to make it clear that Ludolph could not have copied John's work. On page 52 of Ludolph's book, at the end of a list of the nobles who had independent jurisdictions in the city of Acre, occurs the name of 'Vaus.' Nowhere else in Ludolph's book is Vaus or its lords alluded to; and even here it seems as though it were apologetically slipped in at the end of the list, where it might easily escape notice. On turning to John of Hildesheim, however, I find a great deal about Vaus. First of all he declares, in chap. i., that he compiled his *Historia trium Regum* from divers books, known only in the East, and from hearing, sight, and relations of others ; in chap. iv. he mentions as his authorities ' books written in Hebrew and Chaldee of the life and deeds and all matters of the three kings, which had been brought from India to Acre by the princes of Vaus, and had been translated there into French, and were kept there in this translation by certain nobles.' Mr. C. Horstman, the editor of ' The Three Kings of Cologne ' for the Early English Text Society, treats these Hebrew and Chaldaic books as a mere fiction, and says nothing about the Lords of Vaus.

Vaus, according to John of Hildesheim's ' History of the Three Kings,' was the highest and grandest mountain in the East. After the successful conquest of the Promised Land by the Israelites the people of India always kept watchmen on Mount Vaus, and it was from them that the three kings first received tidings of the rising of the star in the East. After the return of the three kings from Bethlehem, when the Apostles separated at the crossways on Mount Sion, St. Thomas went to India, where he baptized the three kings, and built a chapel on Mount Vaus. At the foot of this mount Melchior, King of Nubia and Arabia, built a great city, named Sewilla, Sezile, Seuwa or Seulla, for the spelling varies. This undoubtedly means Saveh in Persia, between Hamadan and Tehran, where Marco Polo 'saw the tombs of the three kings.'[1] The story goes on to tell us that the three kings became priests, and had therefore no direct progeny, but endowed some of their relatives, who called themselves Princes of Vaus, with lands and islands. One branch of the family of these Princes of Vaus came to Acre shortly before its fall, and built itself a castle there. These Princes of Vaus bore a star and a cross in their arms, and John of Hildesheim declares that some of them were present at the court of Rome as ambassadors in the year 1351.

I have been unable to find any mention of the Princes of Vaus in any writer anterior to Ludolph. The name is not uncommon in England ; for example, a Sir John de Vaus sat in Parliament as knight of the shire for Notts in the time of Edward I. There was an Edward Vausse at Cuckfield, in Sussex, in 1595 ('Miscellanea Genealogica et Heraldica,' 1890-91, vol. ii., p. 12). G. Vaus witnessed a marriage in Chester Cathedral, October, 1682. Ursula Vaus, of Odiham, married one of the Coles of Enniskillen. But none of these bore the cross and star in their arms, and none of them seem to have known of the wondrous pedigree which their name entitled them to claim ; they mostly trace to De Vallibus, who came over with the Conqueror, a descent which is commonplace by comparison.

I cannot believe that John of Hildesheim invented the legend of the Lords of Vaus ; but, on the other hand, I cannot find any ground for it. In M. Rey's excellent and

---

[1] Chap. xxx. In the Middle Ages this city was identified with the Saba of Ps. lxxii. 10 : ' The kings of Tharsis and of the isles shall give presents ; the kings of Arabia and Saba shall bring gifts,' which verse was considered to be a prophetical allusion to the three kings.

painstaking reprint of Du Cange's ' Familles d'Outre Mer,' I can find no ' Seigneurs de Vaus,' and though I have spent some time in trying to trace the story, I have not succeeded in so doing.

Felix Fabri was familiar both with John of Hildesheim and with Ludolph. He mentions the latter by name (i. 535), and alludes to the former (i. 637). Moreover, he has reproduced all the gossip about the sea and sea-monsters, islands, etc., which we find in Ludolph's early chapters.

I may add that Robinson (' Palestine,' I. xxiii.), says of Ludolph's work that it is ' decidedly the best *Itinerarium* of the fourteenth century.'

AUBREY STEWART.

LONDON, 1895.

CONTENTS.

LUDOLPH VON SUCHEM'S
DESCRIPTION OF THE HOLY LAND

HERE beginneth Ludolph's book of the pilgrimage to the Holy Land.

Dedicated with all due respect and honour to the Right Reverend Father and Lord in Christ, his gracious Lord Baldwin of Steinfurt, Bishop of Paderborn, by Ludolph, rector of the parish church at Suchem,[1] in the diocese of Paderborn.

Many men write at exceeding great length about the countries beyond the sea, and about the state and condition of the Holy Land and the provinces thereof, after having only passed through them once. Now, I have dwelt in those parts for an unbroken space of five years, being both by day and by night in the company of kings and princes, chiefs, nobles and lords. Having, moreover, many times visited and journeyed through the parts beyond the sea, I have, out of respect and honour for your fatherly goodness, and because you were not forgotten by me—I

---

[1] Some authorities spell this place Sudheim. In the Friburg MS., partially edited by Sir T. Phillipps in 1825, the place is spelled Suchen, and the writer's name appears as Peter instead of Ludolph. The position of Suchem or Sudheim is not known.

have, I say, long desired to write an account of the position
of those countries, their condition, their villages, strong
places, cities, castles, men, manners, places of prayer and
wonders ; and not only to write about the lands beyond the
seas, but also of the wonders which are beheld in the sea
by those who cross over the same. Although heretofore
unable to accomplish this my desire, being hindered by
divers and sundry labours, yet I have ever kept the thought
of this writing in my mind, and being now more at leisure,
I have determined to describe throughout the condition in
which I found the parts beyond sea in the year of our
Lord 1336, and the condition wherein I left them in the
year 1341, and to write a compendious history thereof
briefly, and according to my humble understanding and
genius and the weakness of my memory. Howbeit, let no
one suppose that I beheld with my eyes each several one
of the things which I intend to put into this book, but that
I have happily extracted some of them from ancient books
of history, and that some things I have heard from the
lips of truthful men, all of which, in whatsoever places they
are written or found, I have decided to trust to the judgment of the discreet reader. Indeed, I should have put in
much more if, when in those parts, I had formed the intention of writing some account of them a little earlier ; and
at this present day I could put in yet more, which I pass
over because of ignorant cavillers and scoffers, lest I should
tell anything which they could not believe, and for which
I should be held by them for a liar ; for to ignorant cavillers
and scoffers, who are not worthy to know anything at all,
everything seems incredible and passing belief. Wherefore because to such persons all good things are unknown,
I have been obliged on their account to leave out many
things which otherwise I should have written down and
put into my book.

I.—OF THE HOLY LAND.

Now, the Holy Land, that is, the Promised Land, which God promised that He would give to Abraham and his seed, is beloved by God, praised by angels, and worshipful to men; for our Lord Jesus Christ deigned to consecrate the same with His most precious blood, to honour it with His presence both in the form of our mortal weakness, and in old times, as we read in Bible history, by the glory of His Godhead and majesty, and furthermore therein to redeem the entire human race from eternal damnation. Yet this land, because of the divers sins of its inhabitants, has been scourged by God with divers scourges. Not only is it now scourged in the time of the Christians, but from old times it has been many times inhabited by divers peoples, and many times lost and retaken by them, as may be read in many histories and in the Bible. Yet Jesus Christ, not unmindful of His glorious Passion, hath corrected the Christians therein with the rod of fatherly chastisement; so that now, when the sins of the Christians shall have been ended, and He hath been pleased to restore the land to us, He will have preserved all their places, cities, villages, castles and shrines, as one may say, unhurt to this day; wherefore they might easily be defended, inhabited, and restored, and brought back to their original state, albeit some places and shrines have been sorely defaced by the Saracens. For, as the eye is the dearest and tenderest part of a man's body, and can endure no foreign substance within itself, so is the Holy Land even as an eye to God, and for that cause He cannot endure unrepented sins therein.

He that would go to the said Holy Land must beware lest he travel thither without leave from the Apostolic Father, for as soon as he touches the shore of the Soldan's

country he falls under the sentence of the Pope, because
since the Holy Land came into the hands of the Soldan, it
was, and remains, excommunicate, as are likewise all who
travel thither without the Pope's leave, lest by receiving
tribute from the Christians the Saracens should be brought
to despise the Church.   For this cause, when any traveller
receives his license to go thither from the Apostolic Father,
besides the leave which is granted him, there is a clause in
the Bull to the effect that he shall not buy or sell anything in
the world, save only victuals and clothes and bodily necessaries, and if he contravenes this he is to know that he has
fallen back again under sentence of excommunication.
There are, however, I have heard, many grounds on which
one may journey thither without leave ; for example, if the
traveller be in religion, if a man's father, mother, or friend
be sick there, or held in captivity, then he may travel
thither without leave, to seek for them or to ransom them, or
when anyone is sent thither to make peace or to arrange
and restore any other good thing.   But to return to my
subject.   Whosoever would journey to the Holy Land
must go thither either by land or by sea.   If he would go
by land, I have heard from some who know it well that
the best way is through Hungary, Bulgaria, and the kingdom of Thrace, but they say that the road is a very tedious
one.   Nevertheless, he who could toil over it in safety
would come by land, and not by sea, to Constantinople.   I
will say somewhat about this city.

II.--CONSTANTINOPLE.

Constantinople is an exceeding beautiful and very great
city.   It measures eight miles in circuit, and is built in the
shape of a triangle of buildings in manner and form like
those of Rome, having two of its sides on the banks of an
arm of the sea, which is called the Arm of St. George, while

the third side lies inland. The city is decorated with sundry and divers ornaments, which were built by the Emperor Constantine, who named it Constantinople. The Greeks at this day call it Bolos.[1] In this city there is a church of wondrous size and beauty. I do not believe that in all the world there is a greater than it, for a ship with all its sails spread could easily turn itself round therein, and I do not dare to write fully about its vastness. This church is consecrated in honour of Sancta Sophia[2] in Greek, which in Latin means 'the Lord's Transfiguration.' It is adorned with many solemn relics of divers sorts, to wit: the seamless coat, one of our Lord's nails (of the cross), the sponge, and the reeds,[3] and it is crowned with other relics of divers saints. In the midst of this church stands a great marble column, whereon is a well-gilt brazen statue of the Emperor Justinian[4] on horseback, adorned with the imperial crown and royal vestments, having in his left hand a golden orb[5] after the imperial fashion, and pointing to the east with his right as a threat to rebels in that quarter. In this church there is also a piece of the pillar whereat Jesus was scourged, and an exceeding great number of bodies of saints and of

[1] Πόλις.

[2] F. Deycks's comment is: 'Es scheint, Ludolf verstand nicht Griechisch.'

[3] W. von Boldinsel, A.D. 1336, saw these relics, and 'the greater part of the cross' as well.

[4] See Procopius, 'De Aedificiis,' in this series, Book I., chap. ii.; also Sir John Maundeville, chap. i., fin. John of Hildesheim declares that the Empress Helena placed the bodies of the Three Kings beneath this statue.

[5] The emblem of sovereign power. Compare John of Hildesheim, chap. xxiii.: 'Pomum autem aureum quod Malchiar cum xxx denarijs optulit quondam fuit Alexandri magni, et totaliter potuit manu includi, mundum significans, quod ex minimis particulis tributorum omnium provinciarum conflari fecit, et ipsum semper manu portavit et velud sua potencia totum mundum manu conclusit; quod pomum in India remansit quando de Perside reversus est,' etc.

Roman pontiffs rest therein. This may be known to be true, because in my own days certain gentlemen came thither from Catalonia and served the Emperor of Constantinople for pay, and when they departed begged the Emperor above all for relics. He granted their prayer, set up as many bodies of saints as they numbered heads, and the gentlemen stood afar off and chose each a body in turn, according to their rank. Every one of them who was deserving thereof obtained an entire saint's body, and all were content and returned to their own country with joy. I do not venture to say any more about the other ornaments of this church. In this city the Emperor of the Greeks continually dwells. He who was Emperor[1] in my time had the sister of Duke Henry of Brunswick for his spouse, and on her death married the daughter of the Count of Savoy. In this city dwells likewise the Patriarch of the Greeks, whom the Greeks obey in all things, even as the Latins obey the Pope, and they make no account of the Apostolic Father, neither do they regard any of his commands save such as please themselves. For since the Greeks became separated from the Church of Rome through heresy, they have chosen this Patriarch, and obey him as Pope even to this day. In Constantinople all such things as bread, meat, fish, and the like are sold as it were for nothing, and nothing is dear there save wine, which is brought thither from Naples. In this city dwell many different nations. There is also much cold weather there, wherefore meat is salted there, which cannot be done elsewhere in Asia because of the heat. There also turbots are caught

---

[1] 'Andronicus III., Palaeologus, Kaiser 1321 bis 1341, war zuerst vermählt mit Agnes (später Irene genannt), der Tochter Herzog's Heinrich's I. und Schwester Heinrich's II. Herzogs von Braunschweig, in 2ter Ehe aber mit Anna, der Tochter des Grafen Amadeus V. von Savoyen.'—Dr. F. Deycks.

and dried, and are exported from thence to all parts of Asia. In this city, also, in the Emperor's old palace, there are some stone cups,[1] which of their own accord fill themselves with water and straightway empty themselves, and again fill themselves and become empty. There are withal great and excellent pearls, in very great quantities and very cheap. The reader should know that once the Emperor of the Greeks and the Greek people bore rule over the whole of Asia, both the greater and the lesser, and had them for their own, but since they have been divided from the Church of Rome by schism, they have almost entirely lost those countries. For sentence hath been pronounced against them that whosoever can take any of them captive may lawfully sell them as though they were cattle, and any Latin who can obtain land (there) by force may lawfully hold the same until they return to the bosom of Holy Mother Church and be converted. Wherefore they have lost exceeding great lands and kingdoms, as you shall be told hereafter.

III.—THE WAY (TO THE HOLY LAND) BY LAND, AND THE KINGDOM OF GARP (ALGARVE).

But to return to my subject, and leaving Constantinople, from it one could go to the Holy Land by land, if travelling were safe through the Turks and Tartars and other hindrances in the way. But by sea from Constantinople one must cross over to the kingdom of Cyprus, as you shall be told hereafter. This way, whereof I have made mention, leads ever northwards by land to Constantinople ; and from Constantinople, if it could be done with convenience and safety, one might go by land over the whole world

---

[1] Fabri, i. 358, mentions these 'shells,' as he calls them, and compares them to the weeping pillars of St. Helena's chapel.

towards the south, wherefore there is no need to go by sea.
In like fashion one ought to be able to go (to the Holy
Land) through Barbary and the kingdom of Morocco, and
the kingdom of Granada ; but the Barbarians will not
suffer the Christians to pass through. Yet Saracens who
dwell in Spain and Arragon pass along this road when
they would visit the courts of their prophet Mahomet,
but Christians cannot pass through these kingdoms, for
these two kingdoms of Morocco and Granada are exceed-
ingly powerful and rich, and are inhabited by Saracens who
care naught for the Soldan, and are ever at odds with the
King of Spain, and ever help the King of Algarve, who is
a Saracen, and whose kingdom lies on the borders of Spain,
on that part of the sea which lies over against the King of
Spain. You must know that on that side of the sea the
kingdom of the Saracens still endures, and is called the
kingdom of Algarve, being exceeding powerful and lying
on the Spanish border, as aforesaid. It has many great
cities and strong places and towns, and I believe that the
King of Garp is more powerful than the Soldan ; for if
need were, he could in half a day have more than a hundred
thousand stout armed men, and it is he who ever has
quarrelled and quarrels at this day with the Kings of Spain
and Castile, as you have often heard and known. Likewise, in the kingdom of Arragon all the towns and cities
have Saracens dwelling in them, in which, nay, in each one
of which, the King has a lofty tower with guards, who
watch lest the Saracens should set any mischief on foot,
and whenever the Governor of any town wishes to force
the Saracens to do anything, he gives them the swine to
feed and drive to pasture, which thing is forbidden by their
law, and by this and other means he forces the Saracens to
do his will.

IV.—BARBARY AND PUGIA.

Barbary is a land which is mostly sand and desert, and they who dwell therein are black Ethiopians. Near Barbary is another small country, not six (? German) miles wide, named Pugia,[1] wherein apes are bred and caught. All the dwellers therein have faces like apes, both men and women, and keep apes in their houses even as in these parts men keep dogs and fowls, and from these apes they breed young ones, which they sell and so make their living. For this cause they geld the young apes, lest any should be bred elsewhere ; yet I have often seen young apes bred in divers parts. It should be noted that between Morocco and Spain the Mediterranean Sea flows out to the ocean through an arm scarce a quarter of a mile in breadth ; wherefore upon one bank there stands a Christian woman and on the other bank a heathen woman washing their clothes, and wrangling and quarrelling with one another.[2] This arm of the sea is called by the inhabitants the Straits of Gibraltar, or the Straits of Morocco.

After one has crossed this little arm of the sea, one could go by land over the whole world to the southward, as I said before, were there no hindrances in the way. It is across this arm of the sea that the Kings of Morocco and Granada come to the help of the King of Garp, for they easily cross over it. As the Mediterranean Sea runs out of the ocean through this arm between Spain and Morocco, even so in the same fashion does the Mediterranean Sea run into the Pontic Sea near the walls of Constantinople, through the arm of the sea which is called 'the Arm of St. George,' which is of the same width as the aforesaid.

---

[1] Bougiah, on the coast of Algeria, in longitude 5° E.

[2] Fabri (vol. i., p. 115) copies this story, and also the stories about *Gulph* and *Grup* and the fishes.

And it should be known that in the Pontic Sea no land is found any more, nor is any known of, save only an island called Cherson, whither St. Clement[1] the Pope was exiled and drowned in the same sea ; and we read that in this sea there is a marble temple, to which a passage is open on the day of his feast ; but at the present day it is not, albeit of old it was so. For the body of St. Clement rests at Rome, and the island is deserted, albeit from it most beauteous and excellent marble is exported. [There[2] is another sea to the east beyond the city of Gara, which is held by the Tartars of Cumana,[3] which sea is called the Caspian. This sea does not join either the ocean, the Mediterranean, or the Pontic Sea by any visible arm. Some declare that it is connected with the Pontic Sea, which is the nearest to it, by an underground passage, and consequently is connected with all the others. This Arm of St. George whereof I have spoken divides Europe from Asia Minor, which is a province of Greater Asia. This arm is commonly called the mouth of Constantinople, because thereon on the European shore stands the noble city of Constantinople, also called New Rome, as aforesaid.]

[1] St. Clement, according to tradition, was the third successor of St. Peter, and suffered martyrdom in the Black Sea, into which he was cast with an anchor fastened to his neck. Presently the waves receded, and the corpse of the saint was found seated in a little chapel, with the anchor still attached to it. His feast-day is November 23.

[2] Only one MS. has this. Deycks thinks it is a later insertion : ' Ubrigens hat Felix Fabri' (Th. I., s. 110) 'diese Stelle benutzt.' See Felix Fabri, i. 116, in this series.

[3] Tartarus de Cumana = Comania. See Jean du Plan de Carpin's account of this country in Charton's ' Voyageurs anciens et modernes ' (Paris, 1851), vol. i., p. 230. See also ' De regno Cumanae' in chap. ii., and in Appendix to Haython's ' Historia Orientalis,' in vol. ii. of the ' Fragmentum ' of Vincent of Beauvais, ed. R. Reineccius, Helmstad, MDLXXXV.

V.—THE MEDITERRANEAN SEA.

The Mediterranean Sea is that over which one sails to the Holy Land, and is called the Mediterranean Sea because it has to the east Asia, whose frontier it forms, to the west and north Europe, and to the south Africa, which countries it separates by its arms. Africa and Europe, I have heard, are divided by a river named Inda,[1] wherein the forty martyrs were drowned, and this same river passes by a certain city named Biterris,[2] and it is called Biterris because it stands between two lands—to wit, Africa and Europe. Its Bishop is called the Bishop of Biterris. The Roman philosophers who divided the world among the Romans built this city long ago in the days of Hannibal, and he built another city close by it, named Narbonne, as though it told good tidings (*narrans bona*), which city is now the capital of Biterrae, and the Bishop is called the Bishop of Narbonne. I have often been in that country. But to return to my subject. You must know that the Mediterranean Sea runs in and out, as you have heard, and ebbs and flows, and without doubt is never still, as may be plainly seen between Calabria and Sicily, between which the sea runs so hard that no sailor dares to sail through without a special pilot, and as may be clearly seen in many other places. It should also be known that the Mediterranean Sea is not in all parts of the same width, but in some places it is wider and in some narrower than in others. It is widest measuring from west towards the

[1] Indre in Berry, says Dr. F. Deycks ; but ' Gallia Christiana ' gives ' Biterrensis ' as the title of the Bishop of Beziers, under the Archbishop of Narbonne.

[2] For Beziers see ' Gallia Christiana,' by Sainte Marthe (Paris, 1705), vol. vi., p. 293. The forty martyrs are generally supposed to have suffered at Sebaste, or Ancyra, in Asia Minor. See 'Acta Sanctorum,' March 9.

east, as in Spain, Galicia, Catalonia, and partly in Provence ; but it is narrower measuring from the west to the east, as in Calabria, Apulia, Naples, Venice, and the neighbourhood of these places.[1]

VI.—THE DIVERS PERILS OF THE SEA.

So he who would go by sea to the Holy Land must or may take ship from whatsoever land, or city, or port, of the same that he may choose, and this matter I leave to his free will. With regard to food also, let him take as much as he can or as he has ; but in general men sailing from the West to the East are wont to make provision of food for fifty days, though when sailing from the East to the West they are wont to provide food for one hundred days, because the ship always flies as it were from west to east with a fair wind, making more way in the night than in the day, and travelling fully fifteen miles in every hour of the day. The reason is that the Western land is always exceeding cold and very windy. On the other hand, the Eastern land is exceeding hot and altogether without wind ; wherefore one sails much slower over the sea when returning than when going thither, and especially because great ships going from the West to the East are wont to return in the months of September and October, but galleys and vessels of that sort begin their voyage thither from hence in August, when the sea is smooth ; for in November, December, and January no vessels can cross the seas because of storms. Howbeit no vessels can, except very seldom, return without toil, peril, fear, and tempest. Of this I am well assured, seeing that I have often been in sundry storms at sea beyond all description [for no man can fully describe, neither would anyone believe that there

[1] I have translated this passage as it stands, but cannot guess its meaning.

can be such unheard-of and exceeding fierce storms at sea]. Indeed, I know it to be true that there is no stone or sand at the bottom of the sea that is not moved, if it can be moved, when the sea rages and raves thus, and this is often proved among islands, where the sea is narrow, where an exceeding great number of stones are cast from one shore to another in storms. Once when a certain man was travelling on the Armenian coast in a galley, a sudden storm arose in the night, whereby they lost three men, and in the morning found the galley covered deeper than the hand could reach with sand cast up by the sea in its rage. As the perils of the sea arise from divers causes, I have thought it well to tell somewhat about them.

VII.—THE PERIL CALLED 'GULPH.'[1]

First of all perils arise from the natural winds, as aforesaid ; and likewise from extraordinary winds which sailors at sea call *gulph*, which proceed from the hollows of mountains, and do not do mischief to ships unless they are very near. In the year of our Lord 1341, on the night of the Sunday whereon *Laetare Jerusalem*[2] is sung, we were sailing from the East and had a very good east wind, so that the vessel, with six sails set, travelled all night as though she were flying ; but in the morning at daybreak as we were sailing toward the Satalian[3] mountains, with the sailors all asleep, this same *gulph* flung the ship with all its sails violently on its side into the sea, so that all the sails were wetted, and the ship ran for a long distance almost upon its side, so that had the ship heeled over a palm's breadth more upon its side, we must all have been

[1] Ital., *colpo di vento.*

[2] The introit which gives its name to the Fourth Sunday in Lent.

[3] Satalia, a city in Asia Minor, the ancient Attaleia in Pamphylia, now Adalia.

drowned.   Howbeit we cut all the ropes and fastenings of
the sails until the ship righted itself somewhat, and so by
the grace of God we then escaped that great peril.

VIII.—THE PERIL CALLED GRUP.[1]

There are also other perils at sea arising from an un-
natural wind, which sailors call *grup*.   It arises from the
meeting of two winds, and sailors easily see it coming.
Yet I have suffered peril from it even on my outward
voyage.   Moreover, there are other perils at sea from
pirates or corsairs, who attack a ship even as men do a
castle.   But this peril has been much allayed since the
city of Genoa has chosen unto itself a Doge.

IX.—THE PERILS OF SHOALS.

There are also other perils at sea, which sailors call
shoals.   In respect of these you must know that the sea is
not of the same depth in every part thereof, for in the sea
there are mountains and rocks, grass and green stuff even
as upon land, and these mountains and rocks are higher in
some places and lower in others.   In some places the
rocks and mountains are scarce covered by a palm or a
cubit of water, and for this cause no one dares to sail to the
south towards Barbary, for many rocks and shoals are to be
found there covered by the water.   These perils are greatly
to be feared at sea.   Moreover in storms it is proved that
grass and green things grow in the sea, for at such times
sundry kinds of grass are found cast up on the shore, and
also coral, whose branches stink when they are cast up
from the bottom of the sea, and are afterwards polished by
master craftsmen.   Corals are at first white and stinking,

[1] ' Das Wort " Grup " ist Italienisch.   Gruppo di vento, ein Wirbel-
wind.'—Dr. F. Deycks.

but by the attraction of the sun on the bottom of the sea where they grow they are made red, and they grow in the fashion of a small bush of one ell in height. When they are thus cast up by the sea in great quantities, men gather them and sell them while yet stinking. I have seen in one house more coral than fifty horses could carry ; I do not dare to say more.

X.—PERILS BY FISH.

Likewise in the sea there are other perils, which, however, rarely befall any save little vessels ; that is to say, perils from great fish. About these you should know that there is in the sea a certain fish which the Greeks call Troya marina,[1] which means sea-swine, which is greatly to be feared by small ships, for this same fish seldom or never does any mischief to great ships unless pressed by hunger. Indeed, if the sailors give it bread, it departs, and is satisfied ; but if it will not depart, then it may be terrified and put to flight by the sight of a man's angry and terrible face. Howbeit, the man must be exceeding careful when he is thus looking at the fish not to be afraid of it, but to stare at it with a bold and terrible countenance ; for if the fish sees that the man is afraid it will not depart, but bites and tears the ship as much as it can. If, however, the man looks boldly and savagely at the fish with an angry countenance, the fish becomes affrighted thereat and departs from the ship. An exceeding notable sailor has told me that when he was a youth he fell into peril with this in a small ship. There was with him in the ship a youth who thought himself exceeding brave and fierce, so that

[1] *Troja marina* is the Italian ; French, *truie de mer ;* German, *das Meerschwein, die Stachelsau,* ein Art der Scorpæna.—Dr. F. Deycks. Fabri, who has copied all this gossip about the sea (i. 125), spells the name of this fish ' Troyp.'

when the fish met him he would not give him bread because of the courage which he thought that he had, but lowered himself down by a rope from the ship to the water to look at the fish with an angry face, as is the custom. But when he saw the fish he was straightway affrighted and shouted to his comrades to pull him up by the rope, and the fish, seeing the man's fright, leaped out of the water as he was being drawn up, and with one bite took off half the man from his belly downwards, and departed from the ship. Yet it is said that this fish is not as long as a man can cast a stone, neither is it broad, but its head is exceeding great and broad, and all the damage which it does to ships it does by biting and tearing them.

I have also heard from another very truthful sailor, who knows almost all the paths of the sea, and who has undergone numberless frightful perils of divers sorts at sea—this same man told me that once near Barbary he was forced by a contrary wind to sail in places where sailing is exceeding perilous, because of the rocks and shoals barely covered by water, while not far from such places no bottom could ever be found at ten thousand ells. Now, while he was thus sailing in these places with the greatest possible fear and danger, it chanced that the ship ran upon a fish which the French call *melar*,[1] who was lurking among the rocks there. The fish, when it perceived the ship coming towards him, thought that it was some great morsel which he could swallow, and opening his mouth gave the ship so strong a bite that, albeit heavily laden, it was nevertheless driven back a long way, and all the people on board were awakened by that bite and shock. When the sailor perceived that the ship had recoiled from something impassable, he cried out to the people of the ship to pray to

---

[1] Possibly from *molaris*. The word does not occur in Littré. See Facciolati's Lexicon, s.v. *Xiphias*.

God for their souls, seeing that there was no hope for their lives, for surely the ship must have struck some great rock. And straightway the mariners, the servants of the ship, went down into the hold, wishing to see where the ship was broken. They found that a fish's tooth, as thick as a beam, and three cubits long, had pierced the ship. They afterwards tried to pull out this part of the tooth with iron instruments, and could not, but with a saw they cut it level with the ship's side. There can be no doubt that the ship would have been broken had not this tooth been so sharp, and so wondrously pierced it. As I was wondering at the length and breadth of such a fish, the same sailor told me not to wonder, because there was in the sea a fish a mile long, which was four thousand six hundred miles (? ells) wide in the narrowest part, and even in a small pond not more than one crossbow-shot wide, fish an ell long are often caught. I have seen three such fishes off Sardinia. They puffed out water with their breath into the air in vast quantity, further than a crossbow could shoot, and made a noise like thunder. Moreover, in my time near the isle of Tortosa, such a fish while chasing other little fishes cast himself up on the dry land, driving a great wave of water before him, and when the water ran back into the sea the fish remained on the dry land, and fed all the dwellers in those parts with his flesh and fat. But not long afterwards, as the sun's heat increased, all that country was poisoned by the stench of the fish as it became putrid, and for a long time the skeleton of the fish could be seen from afar like a great house overset with rafters sticking up in the air, but after awhile was carried down lower by storms and squalls. And I have heard from many men of knowledge that there is an exceeding long eel in the sea.

XI.—DIVERS FISHES.

Likewise in the sea there are very many kinds of fishes of divers sorts, both great and small, of sundry colours, appearance, shape, and arrangement, some with scales and some without, the nature of all of which cannot be understood by the human mind. Among these fishes of all sorts there are some which are exceeding wondrous, who lift themselves a long way up out of the water, but level with it, and withal fly for a long distance like bats ; but I am not sure how far they can fly.

I have diligently inquired of knowing seamen whence these fish come, and they have answered me that in England and Ireland there grow on the sea-shore exceeding beauteous trees, which bear fruit like apples. In these apples there is bred a worm, and when the apples are ripe they fall to the ground, are broken in the fall, and the worms fly out, having wings like bees. Those of them who first touch the land become creatures of the air, and fly about with the other fowls of the heavens ; but such worms as first touch the water become creatures of the water, and swim like fish, but yet sometimes wander into the other element and exercise themselves by flight. Whether they do so grow upon trees I do not know beyond having heard the story; but they are eaten like fish, and are seen to fly by men voyaging at sea.

XII.—MIGRATION OF BIRDS.

You must also know that in due season a vast number of birds of all sorts, great and small, journey across the sea from the west to the east and back again, more especially cranes, quails, and swallows, and countless other birds of all sorts and colours, great and small, whose names and numbers God alone knows. They fly from island to island on their way, and are so lean that they are nothing but bones and feathers, and so weary that they care not for stones or arrows. I have caught quails . . . on board ship, but they straightway died. Yet in all the parts in which I have been beyond the seas, I have never seen a stork ; but once in a monastery of Minorites I saw a stork which was held to be a wonder for size. Likewise I have often been asked about swallows, whether they wintered in my country. I said 'No,' but that in my country they came in March, even as they did there, and no one knows from whence they come. Now, it befell that once upon a time, in some great lord's palace, the steward was sleeping upon a table, when there came two swallows quarrelling about a nest, and clinging to and biting one another, so that they both fell upon his face as he slept. He thereupon awoke, caught both the swallows on his face, and held them fast. He then bound a girdle round each of them, and let them fly away, and they came back every year with those same girdles to their nests. I could tell exceeding long stories about other sorts of birds, both great and small, who at their own times cross the sea, but must return to my subject and write no more about such matters.

XIII.—The Voyage across the Sea ; Troy, and the Islands.

Whosoever, then, would visit the Holy Land, or the parts beyond the sea, must travel thither in a ship or a galley. If he travels in a ship, then he passes straight across the sea, not putting into any port, unless forced so to do by contrary winds, want of food, or some such matter of prime necessity, and so he leaves Barbary on his right hand toward the south, and leaves Greece on his left hand toward the north. He gets a distant view of many famous islands, to wit, Corsica, Sardinia, Sicily, Manta, Goy, Scarpe, Crete, Rhodes, and very many other islands, both great and small, and after seeing all these he arrives at Cyprus. But if he crosses in a galley, you must understand that a galley is a sort of oblong vessel which journeys from one shore to another, from one port to another, keeping ever close to the beach, and always putting into harbour ashore for the night. It has sixty benches on either side, and to each bench belong three sailors with three oars, and one archer. On board of a galley fresh provisions are always eaten, which cannot be done on a ship. Now, while the galley is journeying thus along the shore, one sees numberless exceeding fair places, cities, towns and castles, and more especially all those places which in a ship are only seen afar off are seen close at hand from a galley and minutely scanned by the eyes. Thus, it may almost be said that in a galley one coasts round the whole of the northern part of the world, as will be seen hereafter. As one is going thus in a galley from place to place, and from port to port, one comes to Constantinople, whereof I have already told you, and after leaving that city one comes down along the shore of Asia Minor to the place where once stood that most noble city Troy, whereof no trace remains visible, unless it be some foundations under water in the sea, and in some places a few stones and some marble columns buried in the earth, which, when found, are carried away elsewhere. For in respect of this you must know that in the city of Venice there is not a stone column or any good cut-stone work which has not been brought thither from Troy. Near the place where Troy once stood a little city has been built, which is called *Ayos Yamos* in Greek, and is inhabited by Greeks. The city of Troy stood upon the sea-shore in the land called Phrygia, and is not very far distant from Calcedonia, but does not seem to have had a good harbour. As one goes on in a galley from Troy one sees the shores of Lombardy, Campania, Calabria, and Apulia, and one comes to an island named Corsica. It was near this island that St. Paul the Apostle was shipwrecked after he had made his appeal unto Caesar when taken prisoner in Judaea, and here it was that in the evening, when sitting by the fire in the inn, he was bitten by a viper and escaped unhurt, as we read in the Acts of the Apostles. On this island there still dwell men who boast that they are of the family of that innkeeper in whose inn these things befell St. Paul. These same people give to men the power of curing with their spittle any who may have been bitten by serpents or asps. When they confer this power upon any man they take a glass full of wine, and drink thereof first, and then put therein a good deal of their spittle, and if he who is offered to drink thereof is seized with loathing, they thereupon mix earth with the wine, and give it to him that would receive this power or grace, saying, ' Receive thou the power and grace bestowed by God upon us and our children, in honour of St. Paul the Apostle, which we in the same name bestow upon you, that whensoever thou shalt be bitten by a serpent, asp, or any other venomous beast, thou mayest with thy spittle be able to cure and heal thyself and no other man ; and this we grant thee without taking reward for the same, and give it to thee for God's sake. In the name of the Father, the Son, and the Holy Spirit. Amen.' Should anyone heal any other man besides himself, he straightway loses the power, but at the time it benefits him who is healed. From this isle of Corsica one sails to Sardinia, an exceeding noble island, of good and fertile soil, abounding in flocks, herds, and dairies, but not with wine, which is brought thither from elsewhere. In this island formerly rested the body of St. Augustine,[1] but the King of the Lombards translated it thence to Pavia. In this island also was born St. Macarius, most notable among hermits. This island once belonged to the Pisans, but the King of Arragon took it from them by force. It does not contain many cities, but has one fine city named Castel de Cal.[2] Near this is a castle named Bonayr.[3] On Ascension Day in the year 1341, we were driven upon this island in an exceeding great ship by a most furious and violent tempest which suddenly arose, so that it took us fifteen days to recover the distance which we ran before the storm from the sixth hour to the time of vespers. The oldest man of modern times remembers no such great storm at sea. The same night that we were driven thither thirty-four other great ships assembled there, which had, like ourselves, been driven thither from divers parts of the sea, and numberless other craft, both great and small, some of which had cast their cargo overboard, and some were damaged. Among all these ships there came the greatest ship in all the world from Naples, laden with a thousand tuns of wine of the largest size, with more than six hundred men and divers kind of merchandise, with which she was bound for Constantinople, but was driven back by the violence of the storm. This island of Sardinia is close to another little isle, called Sauper, that is to say, St. Peter's Isle,[4] whereon

---

[1] St. Augustine's body was brought from Hippo in 506 (he died there in 430) to Sardinia, and from thence was brought by King Luitprand in 725, first to Genoa, and then to Pavia, where King Luitprand built the church of St. Peter and St. Augustine, called Cielo d'Oro. A monument to these saints was later erected in the cathedral.

[2] Calaris, Cagliari.

[3] Bonaria.

[4] There is a little island called San Pietro off the south-west coast of Sardinia.

there are wild horses, exceeding small and of great beauty, which for their swiftness cannot be taken, save that by stealth they are shot with arrows and eaten for venison. Between this island and Provence the sea is exceeding dangerous, and this place is called by sailors Gulph de Leun, which is, being interpreted, 'the lion's rage.' For though a ship may have sailed peacefully over all the rest of the sea, yet it never crosses this arm of the sea without great storms, dangers and alarms, wherefore this same place is called Gulph de Leun. From this island of Sardinia men sail to the island of Sicily, a most noble country measuring eighty miles round about. This is an exceeding good kingdom, and this island is fertile beyond all the neighbouring countries, for when by failure of rain there is dearth in all lands and parts beyond the sea, they are fed and helped by Sicily alone.

XIV.—THE ISLAND OF SICILY.

This kingdom of Sicily hath within it seven bishoprics and one metropolitan—to wit, he of Monreal, who in my time was a Minorite friar. Moreover, it has very many exceeding strong and noble cities, fortalices, and towns, and especially most beauteous and strongly fortified cities on the sea-shore, all of them with good harbours—to wit, Messina, Palermo, Trapani, and Catania. In the city of Catania dwell Dominican friars, who have a painting of the Blessed Mary at the time of the Annunciation, which the people of the city greatly reverence, as do also those who sail upon the sea, for no ship passes within a certain distance thereof without greeting and visiting this picture, and they tell one, and firmly believe, that if any ship were to pass by without greeting or visiting the picture, it would not reach home without meeting with a storm. In the city

of Catania St. Agatha suffered martyrdom, and her entire
body rests there, and is greatly reverenced and most carefully
guarded, for because of her merits God daily works many
miracles throughout Sicily. Near this city of Catania
there stands by itself an exceeding lofty mountain, which
they who dwell there call Mount Bel[1]—that is to say, the
Beautiful Mountain. This mountain never ceases to flame
and smoke like a fiery furnace, and casts forth burned
stones of the size of a small house, which the people of
these parts call pumice-stone, wherewith parchment is
smoothed. This and other rubbish cast out by the mountain has been collected and heaped together by the wind
till it has formed what may almost be called great and
long mountains. It was from this mountain that there
came forth the river of fire whereof we read in the Passion
of St. Agatha, where it is said, ' They set up an awning to
keep off the fire.' The course of this river may be clearly
seen at the present day ; howbeit the like river of fire has
often flowed out since the time of St. Agatha, and even
now sometimes flows out. Indeed, a great part of Sicily
is laid waste by these rivers of fire and the pumice-stone
cast forth from the mountain, for when the rivers cool they
harden, and cannot be broken up by irons or any tools
whatsoever. It is said that in that mountain is hell's
mouth, and no doubt there is something in this story, for
it has been proved and decided by many voices, miracles,
and examples, both at the present day and in the ancient
histories of the kingdom ; for whenever there are any great
battles anywhere, this same mount sends forth flames as
high as heaven itself, and thereupon they who dwell in
Sicily know that there are of a truth battles being fought
in some parts of the world. A Minorite friar who had
dwelt for a long time in Sicily told me that of his own

---

[1] Mongibello, Ætna, so called from the Arabic *Gebel*.

knowledge, when the Emperor Henry[1] of blessed memory and the Pisans were fighting against King Robert in Mount Cachym,[2] in which war King Robert's brother was slain, and lies buried in Pisa at this day beneath the sepulchre of the aforesaid Emperor, that this mount flamed so brightly that all through the night of the battle the Dominican monks in Messina, which is twenty miles distant from the mount, read their matins by the light of the flames. He declared that the same thing had befallen himself when there was a battle between the Florentines and Perusians at Altpas (Alepas). This friar told me many other wondrous stories of this mount, which would take long to tell. For this cause there is a common proverb in Sicily, ' I had rather be in Mount Bel with kings and princes than in heaven with the halt and blind ;' and the meaning is clear, for here the men are utterly vile, but the women are most admirable. In Sicily they practise three rites indifferently : in one part they follow the Latin rite, in another that of the Greeks, and in another that of the Saracens ; yet they are all Christians, albeit they differ and disagree in their rites. It is a great wonder that Sicily can be so fertile and charming a country when it so often suffers such terrible damage from this mountain ; for sometimes it happens that this mountain casts forth so much ashes in one or two days, that the flocks cannot for a long time find any pasture. Moreover, sometimes so many rivers of fire and flames and other dreadful things come forth from the mountain, that they who dwell there

[1] Henry VII. of Luxemburg died 1313. His monument stands at the west end of the Campo Santo at Pisa. See John of Winterthur's chronicle in Eccard's ' Corpus Historicum Medii Aevi,' vol. i., p. 1775.

[2] There was a battle on *Monte Catini* on August 29, 1315, where Ugguccione dello Faggiuola, the Ghibelline Prince of Pisa and Lucca, defeated the Florentines and the troops of Robert of Apulia. I conclude that this is what is meant.

fast and make vows, expecting that they will be taken down
quick into hell. These rivers come out of the mountain like
red-hot glowing brass, and (the fire) consumes everything
which it finds on its way, whether it be wood or stones,
even as hot water consumes snow, and lays waste the land
in some places for a distance of two miles, according as the
land is high or low, making it a desert and for ever un-
inhabitable, wherefore albeit Sicily is an exceeding good
land, yet it is a fearful thing to dwell therein.

XV.—THE MOUNT VULCAN.

Likewise near Sicily there is another small island having
only one mountain in it, at the foot of which mount there
is a most beauteous and delightful orchard. This mount
is called Vulcan by the inhabitants, and it suddenly, like a
furnace, pours forth blazing flames in much more horrible
fashion than Mount Bel. This mount, we read, once stood
in Sicily, but by the merits of the Apostle St. Bartholomew
cast itself into the sea and removed itself from the land.
It flames most exceeding terribly and violently, and casts
forth pumice-stones of the size of small houses into the air
like a catapult, with such force that they burst in the air
like apples, and pieces fall into the sea for half a mile
round about, and are cast up on the beach by the waves
and gathered there. This is the pumice-stone which
scribes use to smooth parchment, which some declare to
be formed from the sea-foam, which is false, as you have
been told. Once before I went to Sicily a lake of fire burst
into the orchard at the foot of Mount Vulcan, and it was
a stone's-throw long and wide, and for four days and
nights flames went forth up to heaven from the length and
breadth of it in so terrible a fashion that all men thought
that of a truth heaven and earth were on fire, and that the
day had come when they should pass away. When the

flames ceased for four more days and nights so many ashes came forth that in many places men deserted their towns and cities and all that they had, and fled into the mountains to shelter themselves from the ashes as best they might, and all the flocks and very many people perished in the plains by the ashes. Many cities, even, could not be seen at all, they were so covered with ashes, and many rivers were dried up by the ashes. There was such sorrow and anguish through Sicily at that time as no man could remember or ancient history tell of. Thereupon the Sicilians vowed vows to God, proclaimed fasts, gave themselves up to works of penitence, and prayed to God that He would turn away His anger from them, and for the sake of the merits of St. Agatha would set them free from so great tribulation. Thereupon straightway the trouble came to an end, and thereafter they felt nothing of the sort. They then forbade upon the highest penalties the doing of many wicked deeds which had heretofore been permitted.

XVI.—THE CITY OF SYRACUSE.

There is also in Sicily another city, which is called Syracuse, wherein St. Lucia suffered martyrdom, and wherein her entire body now rests ; and there are numberless other venerable relics of saints. It would be too long for me to tell you of the other wonders of Sicily, and of the glories and palaces of the Emperor Frederick, the catching of the fish called tunny, and its other sources of wealth and abundance.

Near Sicily there are many other islands, both great and small, inhabited by Saracens. Near it there is also another island called Malta, containing one bishopric, which I have often visited in passing. Near it there is another island named Colmat, whereon there are so many rabbit-holes that the people have hardly land enough left to live upon. Near it is another small island named Scola ; no one visits these little islands except he be on a special journey to them. Near these, too, is another island called Goy (Gozo), which abounds in flocks and dairy produce. Once I sailed between this and the other island with great peril in a great ship during a most violent storm, and no one remembered so great a ship to have ever gone through that way.

XVII.—ACHAIA.

Proceeding from Sicily, one sails across the Venetian Gulf, which divides Italy from Greece, and coasting round the shores of Greece, one comes to Achaia and Macedonia and other parts of Greece, which are called Romania. You must know that the land which used to be called Achaia is now called Morea. The Catalonians have reft this land from the Greeks by force. Therein is a fair city named Patras, wherein the Apostle St. Andrew suffered martyrdom. Moreover, St. Antony and many other saints once dwelt there or were born there. Not far from Patras is Athens, wherein once flourished the schools of the Greeks. This was once an exceeding noble city, but now is almost deserted ; for there is scarce anywhere in Genoa a marble column or piece of good hewn stone which has not been brought thither from Athens, and the whole city is built out of Athens, even as Venice is built of the stones of Troy. In this same land of Achaia there is the most beauteous and strong city of Corinth, standing on the top of a mountain, the like of which city has scarce ever been heard of for strength ; for were the whole world to besiege it, it never would lack for corn, wine, oil, and water. It was to this city that St. Paul wrote several epistles. Not far from Corinth stands the city of

Galatas, to which also St. Paul wrote epistles. *Gala* in Greek means the same as *lac* (milk) in Latin ; for they who dwell therein are whiter than the other people round about, from the nature of the place, and this city, which once was called Galatas, is now called Pera. Moreover, in Achaia, or Morea, there dwell brethren of the house of the Germans,[1] who have there exceeding strong castles, and are ever at variance with the Duke of Athens and the Greeks. As one goes on from Achaia or Morea one comes to sundry Greek isles in sailing along the shore of Asia Minor, and one arrives at an island named Syo,[2] which is a specially notable isle. Therein grows mastic, and nowhere else in the world, for though trees thereof grow well enough elsewhere, yet no fruit is found upon them. Mastic grows like gum, dropping from the trees, and from hence is sent all over the world. This island has a Bishop, who in my time was of the Dominican Order. This island was forcibly reft from the Emperor of Constantinople by two Genoese brothers, and afterwards these two brothers fell out, and one of them secretly gave back his part to the Emperor, took his brother prisoner, and kept him for a long time in prison, and the Emperor took the island away from both of them ; but in my time he took the captured brother into his favour, made him the commander of his army, and gave him some castles. From Syo one sails to the desert isle of Patmos, whither St. John the Evangelist was exiled by Domitian, and where he saw the heavens open, and wrote the Book of Revelation. From Patmos you can sail on to the coast of Asia Minor and come to Ephesus, if you please. This land, which once was called Asia Minor, is now called Turkey, for the Turks have taken it from the Greeks. You must know

[1] ? The Teutonic Order. Cf. Fabri, i. 185.
[2] Chios.

that the Turks are tall black men and most zealous
Saracens, yet not of the Saracen race, but rather renegade
Christians. They are in all respects like the Frisians, and
dwell by the northern (*sic*) sea-shore in exceeding strong
castles which they have taken from the Greeks, having no
arms but bows and arrows, living on milk and the like,
wandering hither and thither with their flocks, in all
respects mean, and with the same customs as Frisians.

XVIII.—THE CITY OF EPHESUS.

You must know that the true city of Ephesus is four
short miles distant from the sea. In this city there is a
fair church built in the form of a cross, roofed with lead,
nobly decorated with mosaic work and marble, and entire
to this day. It was here that the beloved disciple,
when bidden to a feast, entered a sepulchre, was over-
shadowed by darkness, and seen no more. This sepulchre
is near the high altar, and the place where it is hewn in a
rock is openly shown, if those who enter will first give a
penny to the Turks. In the church the Turks now sell
silk, wool, corn, and the like merchandise. The city of
Ephesus once stood in a strange fashion between two hills,
so that it had its outskirts upon mountains and its midst
in a valley. The church wherein is St. John's sepulchre
was a crossbow-shot distant from this city, and stood on
the top of a mountain. But as the ground near the church
was stronger, the city of Ephesus has been removed by the
Turks through fear of the Christians, and the old city is
now deserted. In my time there dwelt there a noble lady
whose husband owned the whole city. There was also
one Zalabin, a Turk, who took away the city from them,
and by whose consent the noble lady dwelt beneath the
castle of Ephesus. She had a license from him to sell

wine to merchants, and with many groans opened to us the sorrows of her heart at the loss of her husband and her city. Near the city of Ephesus there is a small round fountain, which contains excellent fish in great numbers. From this fountain water bursts forth in such quantity that all the meadows and orchards and the whole land is watered thereby. You must know that the city, which once was called Ephesus, was afterwards called Theologos[1] by the Greeks, and is now called Altelot, that is, High Place (*altus locus*), because, as I have already told you, the city has been removed to a higher place round about the church. About four miles from this ancient town of Ephesus a new city has now been built, on the sea-shore at a place where there is a harbour, and it is inhabited by Christians who have been driven out of Lombardy through a quarrel. These people have churches and Minorite friars, and live like Christians, albeit they did in former times together with the Turks do great injury to Christian people. Near the new city of Ephesus there is a river as large as the Rhine, which runs down through Turkey from Tartary. By this river much merchandise of divers sorts is brought down, even as is done on the Rhine in these parts. It is in this river that the Turks and Christians falsely so called, when they have a mind to fight against the Christians, are wont to collect their ships, arms, and provisions, so that from this river much harm and damage has come to the Christians.

[1] 'The modern name of *Ayasaluk* is a corruption of *Agios Tzeologos*, an epithet which the modern Greeks apply to St. John, the founder of the Ephesian Church.'—Arrowsmith's 'Eton Geography.'

'Ephesus,' says Mrs. S. S. Lewis, 'is called Ayassoulouk, a Turkish name derived, perhaps, from the Greek Agios Theologos, but called by the mediaeval Italians Alto Luogo, the High Place. — 'A Lady's Impressions of Cyprus;' Remington, 1894.

XIX.—THE DIFFERENT ISLES OF THE SEA, AND FIRST OF ALL, RHODES.

From Ephesus one sails onward to many other different isles. You must know that in that part of the sea there are more than seven hundred isles, both great and small, inhabited and desert, many of which have many special virtues, and some of which abound with all manner of good things, while some are full of poisonous springs and exceeding venomous creatures. Among these isles there is one small one, which has a fount of very hot water, boiling like a pot, and so poisonous that a bird dies if it only flies over it. Near this isle is another isle, scarce measuring two miles in circuit, whereon stands a little church. On this isle there are stags and other wild animals, so that the isle has scarce room for them. Once my comrades landed on this isle, and found in the church lances, shields, cross-bows, very many arms, and great store of dried meat, which was brought thither by pirates and sea-robbers as they took it from time to time, and laid it up there. My comrades waited there all day expecting the robbers to come ; they also went hunting without catching any-thing. But it chanced towards evening that one of them was sitting between two rocks, and a stag happening to come upon him, he cut off its right foot and wounded the left with one blow of his sword ; so they got the stag, and departed. Near this isle is another, wherein there are are no animals save wild asses, which are exceeding good sport to hunt, but have not good meat to eat like other beasts of chase. Not far from this isle there is another named Peyra, a very good one, wherein are found three forms of the stone called *alun*, in exceeding great quan-tity, so that it is exported from thence to all the world. Not long ago the Genoese took this island from the Turks by force, and have well restored it and its bishopric into its original state. This island is near Turkey, and between them there is a bridge, over which the Turks will not, if they can help it, allow anyone to pass, whether there be peace or war between them, so vexed are they at the loss of the island. It is too long to tell you about the other isles. Leaving all these, one sails back again to the shore of Asia Minor or Turkey, and comes to Patara,[1] which once was a noble and most beauteous city, but now has been destroyed by the Turks. In this city the pious Pope St. Nicholas[2] was born. One sails on from Patara, and comes to another once most noble city, but now destroyed, named Mirrhea,[3] wherein the glorious Pope Nicholas, who has illustrated all that country by his many miracles and virtues, was wondrously elected Bishop.[4] From Mirrhea, if you choose, you can sail on, and you will come to an exceeding good and notable isle named Crete, which once was a kingdom in itself, but which does not contain many forts or cities. Its greatest city is named Candia. In the greater part of this isle sage is burned for firewood. The Venetians have taken this isle by force from the Greeks. From Crete one sails to another most fair and notable isle, which is healthy and pleasant. It was once called Colos,[5] and has a Metropolitan who is called Colossensis.

[1] See Sir John Maundeville, chap. iv.

[2] There have been five Popes of this name, but the Bishop of Myrrha was not one of them.

[3] Myra in Lycia.

[4] ' Comme le dit Jacques de Varazze, les prelates du voisinage étaient venus pour donner un successeur à l'évêque de Myre, et l'un d'eux apprit du Ciel qu'il fallait sacrer le premier qui se presenterait le matin à la porte de l'église. Ce fut Nicolas, qui venait faire sa prière sans se doubter de rien.'—'Caracteristiques des Saintes dans l'Art Populaire,' par le Père Ch. Cahier, S.J., Paris, 1867, art. ' Bourse.'

[5] See Sir John Maundeville, chap. iv., and Wright's note ; also Saewulf. St. Paul's Colossae was a city in the upper part of the basin of the Maeander, on one of its affluents called the Lycus.

It was to this isle that St. Paul wrote his Epistles (to the Colossians). Now the isle is called Rhodes, because of the seventh climate of the world, wherein that isle stands alone, and divides and marks the climate.[1]

It was from this isle that first came the destruction of the noble city of Troy, for they say that there lived the ram with the golden fleece, of whom one reads at greater length in the histories of Troy. This isle of Rhodes is an exceeding precious one, being mountainous, and standing in a very healthy air, abounding in the wild animals called fallow-deer. Furthermore, from whatever part of the sea you sail you must pass by or near Rhodes. In this isle there is a city named Rhodes, exceeding beauteous and strong, with high walls and impregnable towers built of such great stones that it is a wonder how human hands can have laid them in their place. When Acon was lost, the Master and brethren of St. John of Jerusalem took this isle by force[2] from the Greeks. They besieged it for years, but they never would have taken the city had they not won over the inhabitants by bribes, so that they delivered up the isle of their own accord. Thereupon the brethren of the Order made it their headquarters, and there they dwell to this day. There are three hundred and fifty brethren and the Master of the Order, who in my time was Elyonus,[3] a very old and very stingy man, who has amassed countless treasure, and built much in Rhodes, and has set the Order free from vast debts. This isle lies within the sound of a man's voice from Turkey, from which it is separated by an arm of the sea, and takes tribute from all the country round about, and from Turkey a third part of

[1] See 'Clima' in Zedler's 'Universal Lexicon.' It seems to be almost equivalent to 'degree of latitude.'

[2] The Grand Master Guillaume de Villaret, after useless negotiations with the Emperor Andronicus II., stormed Rhodes 1310.

[3] Helion de Villeneuve, Grand Master 1327-1346.

the produce of the land. It has also a small and exceeding strong castle in Turkey.[1] These brethren have a truce with the rest of the Turks on land, but not at sea, nor yet in places where they are harming the Christians. These same brethren of the Hospital hold also another island hard by named Lango,[2] abounding in corn, wine, oil, and many fruits, and therein dwell fifty brethren from Rhodes. The brethren have yet another small isle, a good and fertile one, named Castelroys,[3] which once was laid waste by the Turks, but now is well inhabited by the brethren and their mercenaries. In it there is an exceeding strong and lofty castle, from which all ships sailing to whatsoever part of the sea can be seen for a distance of almost fifty miles, and then they make signals to the brethren in Rhodes and Lango and to the other Christians round about, with smoke by day and with flames by night, telling them how many ships there are at sea, whereupon the brethren and Christians make preparations for battle and defence according to the number of ships signalled. This island

[1] In 1344 the Knights took the fort and part of the town of Smyrna from the Turks, and held their conquest for fifty-six years. Ludolph wrote in 1350, and probably alludes to this.

[2] Cos. See Wright's note to Sir John Maundeville, in Bohn's 'Early Travels in Palestine.'

[3] This is the modern island of Kastelorizo, called by the Italians Castel Rosso, the ancient Cisthene, or Megiste (Liv., xxxvii. 22, 24), near Patara, at the south-west angle of Asia Minor. But an article on the Knights of Malta in the *Penny Magazine*, vol. v., p. 246, says : ' On the summit of a mountain in the island of Syme, Fulk de Villaret had erected a lofty tower whence ships could be discovered at a great distance. As soon as a strange sail was signalled, which was done by lighting fires at night and making a dense smoke by day, the pinks and light frigates of Syme, the row-boats and galleys of Rhodes, the feluccas and light and swift vessels of others of the islands, got under weigh,' etc. Syme is a small island between Rhodes and the promontory of Budrun (Halicarnassus). Leake ('Tour in Asia Minor,' 1824) mentions Castelorizo. See his note on p. 184.

is exceeding useful to the Christians, for since the brethren
have held the island and castle, the Turks have done the
Christians no harm with their ships.   Moreover, before the
time of the brethren the islands of Rhodes and Lango, and
all the isles and country of the Christians round about,
used to pay tribute to the Turks, but now by the grace of
God the brethren have turned this the other way.   When
the Turks first heard that the isle of Rhodes had been
conquered by the brethren of St. John, they collected a
great army, and sent a solemn embassy asking at first in
bland and pacific terms for the tribute due to them from
the brethren, and declaring that they would willingly make
peace and a treaty with the brethren, but that in any case
they must have their tribute.   At that time the Order had
no Master, for Brother Fulco de Villaret,[1] the Master of the
Order, had been deposed by the brethren through a quarrel.
But a certain brother from Basle, a very brave and honest
knight, who was at that time Guardian of the Order, made
answer to the Turks begging for a space of three days for
consideration, and a truce for that time, which the Turks
most willingly granted, and charged their army to observe.
Meanwhile this same Guardian of the Order daily continued
to feast with the Turks, and cunningly found out all about
their army, its state and position, and what it intended to
do ; in the meanwhile he got together as many ships and
men as he could, and on the third day, pretending that he
was about to leave Rhodes to fight against the Greeks, he
asked the Turkish ambassadors to enter his chamber lest
any evil should befall them at the hands of the Christians
until his return.   The ambassadors did this, and that knight,
the Guardian of the Order, after having set guards over
them who were in his secret, embarked with his army and

---

[1] Grand Master Fulke de Villaret was elected A.D. 1308, was
deposed 1321, and died 1327.

put out to sea. At dawn on the morrow he fell upon the host of the Turks, and slew them all without distinction, men and women, young and old alike. For it is the habit of the Turks and Tartars to take their wives, their little ones, and all their property with them in their army whithersoever they march. So after they had slain all the people and won all their property and flocks, the brethren returned to Rhodes on the third day with great joy. I have heard from some who were present that they got so much plunder that they towed their spoils behind the ships by ropes in the sea. When all this had been arranged and settled, the Guardian of the Order called forth the Turkish ambassadors, and said to them that the brethren were willing to make a truce and treaty with the Turks, and straightway sent them away; and they on the same day landed with great joy at the place where they had left their army. But they found all their army newly slain, the bodies stripped and plundered, and all the property carried off. When they beheld this, they went home as sorrowful as they had been joyful, and brought the news to the rest of the Turks. Thenceforth the Turks and Tartars have never asked the brethren of St. John or the Christians in Rhodes for tribute even to this day. At Rhodes there are also many venerable relics, among which is a brazen cross, which is believed to be made out of the basin wherein Christ washed the disciples' feet. Wax moulds of this cross have great power in quelling storms at sea. This cross and some other venerable relics of the brethren of St. John once belonged to the Templars, all of whose goods and castles are now owned by the aforesaid brethren. It would take too long to tell of the other glories of Rhodes, and of all the several victories of the aforesaid brethren. From Rhodes one sails to Cyprus.

XX.—CYPRUS.

Cyprus is an exceeding noble and famous, and also an exceeding rich isle, beyond comparison with all the other isles of the sea, and is fertile in all good things beyond the rest. It was, we read, first inhabited by Noah's son Japhet, and for its size it excels all the other lands and seaside cities round about, being encircled as it were with a girdle by the countries of Egypt, Syria, Armenia, Turkey, and Greece. From Cyprus to all these is not more than a day's journey by sea, as you shall hear hereafter. This glorious island once belonged to the Templars, who sold it to the King of Jerusalem. Then, when Acre and the Holy Land were lost and ruined, the King of Jerusalem, and the princes, nobles and barons of the kingdom of Jerusalem, removed to Cyprus and dwelt there, and there they abide to this day, and thus Cyprus became a kingdom. In Cyprus there are three bishoprics—to wit, Paphos, Limasol, and Famagusta, and one Metropolitan, the Bishop of Nicosia, who in my day was a Minorite friar named Elias, who was made a cardinal by Pope Clement VI.[1] The oldest city in Cyprus is Paphos, once a very noble and great place, but now it is almost ruined by continual earthquakes. It stands on the seashore directly over against Alexandria. Paul and Barnabas converted[2] this city to faith in Christ, and from thence the whole earth hath been converted to the faith, as is set forth in the Acts of the Apostles. Near Paphos once stood Venus's[3] Castle, where they used to worship the idol Venus, and travel from distant lands to visit her gates, and thither all noble lords and ladies and young damsels

---

[1] Pope 1342-1353.
[2] Acts xv. 39.
[3] The ' Venusberg ' of the Tannhäuser legend

gathered together in that castle. It was in this temple that the first step was taken towards the ruin of Troy; for Helen was taken when on her way to this temple. Moreover, all damsels and girls used to make vows in this temple for marriage and husbands, wherefore in Cyprus men are lustful by nature beyond those of all other lands, for if earth from Cyprus, and more especially from the place where Venus's Castle used to stand, be placed beneath a man's head as he sleeps, it will throughout the whole night dispose him to lust. Near Paphos is the place where St. Hilary used to dwell, and where he wrought many miracles, and there are many other places wherein many other saints used to dwell, especially St. Zyzonimus and St. Mamma, who was born in Germany, and it is to him that the Greeks are commonly wont to pray most devoutly for deliverance from carbuncles.

XXI.—THE VINEYARD OF ENGADDI.

In this same diocese of Paphos is the vineyard of Engaddi, the like of which is not in the world. This vineyard stands upon an exceeding lofty mountain,[1] two miles long. A tall cliff girds it on every side like a wall; it has one exceeding narrow entrance, and is quite flat on the top throughout. In this vineyard grow many grapes and vines of divers sorts, some of which yield grapes as big as great pears, and some yield grapes as small as peas. Some vines yield bunches of grapes as big as urns, and others

[1] Probably the promontory which terminates in Cape Gatto, the ancient Kyrias, near Limasol. This was the district which produced the wine called 'Commanderia.' It was guarded by the castle of Kolossin, the headquarters of the Hospitallers in Cyprus, wherein are the arms of the Lusignans, quartering Jerusalem, Armenia, and Cyprus, between three other coats, being those of Antoine Fluvian, Grand Master of the Hospitallers 1421-1437, of Jacques de Milli, Grand Master 1454-1461, and another which has not been identified.

exceeding small bunches, and some vines yield white grapes, some black, and some red ; some vines yield grapes without stones, and some oblong grapes, shaped like acorns, and transparent; and countless other sorts of vines and grapes are to be seen in this vineyard. This vineyard once belonged to the Templars, but now belongs to the brethren of the Hospital of St. John at Rhodes. In the time of the Templars there were always a hundred slaves— that is, Saracen prisoners—there always, who had no duties or work imposed upon them save dressing and tending the vineyard. I have heard from many men of great experience that there is no more beauteous, noble, or wondrous gem under the sun than this, which God hath made for the use of man, like as we read of the same in Solomon's Song : ' My beloved is unto me as a cluster of camphire[1] in the vineyards of Engaddi.'

Not far from Paphos is Limasol, once a fair city, but now much damaged by earthquakes and sudden rushes of water from the mountains. This city stands on the sea-shore directly over against Tyre, Sidon, and Beyrout. When Acon was lost, the Templars and Hospitallers of St. John and other nobles dwelt in this city, and many of their palaces and castles may be seen at this day. Near Limasol is another vineyard, called Little Engaddi, wherein grow divers vines, which a man cannot span with his arms, but they are not very tall, and do not yield much fruit. In a place in this diocese called Pravimunt (Peninunt) dwell brethren of the Teutonic Order, and also Englishmen of the Order of St. Thomas of Canterbury. There is also in this diocese an exceeding lofty mount,[2]

---

[1] 'Botrus Cypri dilectus meus in vinea Engaddi,' in the Vulgate (Cant. i. 14, iv. 13), where the allusion is not to the island of Cyprus, but to the plant cypress ($\kappa\acute{\upsilon}\pi\rho o s$).

[2] S. Croce, the modern Stavrovuni, near Larnaca. See Fabri, i. 193-200.

standing by itself, much like Mount Tabor, on whose top stands a fair monastery, wherein are brethren of the Order of St. Benedict. In this monastery is the entire cross whereon the thief on Christ's right hand hung, which was brought thither by St. Helena, by whom also this monastery was built and endowed. This cross is devoutly greeted by all mariners at sea when they draw near to this mount, and God works many miracles on the mount by reason of the virtues of the said cross. Mount Lebanon can always be clearly seen from this mount.

XXII.—THE CITY OF FAMAGUSTA.

The third city of Cyprus is called Famagusta. It stands on the sea-shore, and there is now the harbour for the whole sea and the whole kingdom, and thither merchants and pilgrims must needs flock together. This city stands directly over against Armenia, Turkey, and Acre. This is the richest of all the cities in Cyprus, and its citizens are exceeding wealthy. Once one of the citizens of Famagusta was betrothing his daughter, and the French knights who were sailing with us reckoned that the jewels she wore on her head were better than all the jewels of the King of France. There was a merchant of this city who sold a royal golden orb[1] to the Soldan for sixty thousand florins. It contained only four precious stones—to wit, a carbuncle, a pearl, a sapphire, and an emerald, and yet he afterwards went and begged to be allowed to buy that orb back again for a hundred thousand florins, but was refused. Moreover, the Constable of Jerusalem had four pearls which his wife wore as a brooch, which whenever and wherever he pleased he could pawn for three thousand florins. In a warehouse in this city there is more aloes-

---

[1] See the chapter on Constantinople.

wood than five carts can carry ; I say nothing about spices, for they are as common there as bread is here, and are just as commonly mixed and sold. Neither dare I say any more about precious stones, cloth-of-gold, and other kinds of wealth, because in those parts there is an unheard-of and incredible store of them. In this city dwell number-less exceeding rich courtesans, some of them possessing more than a hundred thousand florins, about whose riches I dare say no more.

XXIII.—SALAMINA AND NICOSIA.

Near Famagusta there is another city on the sea-shore named Constantia or Salamina, which once was an exceed-ing noble, famous, and beauteous city, as its ruins bear witness. In this city a man of wondrous sanctity, St. Epiphanius,[1] was miraculously elected Bishop, and is buried therein. In the same city was born St. Katharine the Virgin, and a chapel stands on the place of her nativity to this day. In this city St. Barnabas the Apostle suffered martyrdom, and near it his body was burned and buried. St. Epiphanius glorified this city and all the country round about with many miracles ; but the city is now utterly ruined. Also in Cyprus there is another exceeding great city named Nicosia. This is the metropolis of Cyprus, and stands in the midst thereof in a plain at the foot of the mountains, and in an exceeding healthy air. The King of Cyprus and all the bishops and other prelates of the kingdom dwell in this city because of the healthiness of the air, and also the greater part of all the other princes, counts, barons, and knights live there, and every day they amuse themselves with joustings, tournaments, and espe-cially with hunting. In Cyprus there are wild rams,

---

[1] Epiphanius, Bishop of Salamis or Constantia, in Cyprus (May 12). I can find nothing strange about his appointment in ' Acta Sanctorum.'

which are not found anywhere else in the world, and they are taken with leopards; they can be taken in no other way. The princes, nobles, barons, knights, and citizens of Cyprus are the richest in the world, for one who has a revenue of three thousand florins is thought less of there than a man who had a revenue of three marks would be in these parts. But they spend it all in hunting. I knew a count of Jaffa who kept more than five hundred hounds, every pair of which dogs, according to the custom of those parts, had a servant of their own, to keep them clean, bathe them, and anoint them, which must needs be done to hunting dogs in those parts. Also another noble keeps at the least ten or twelve falconers, with special wages and their expenses. I have known many nobles and knights in Cyprus who could have kept and maintained two hundred armed men for less than they paid for their huntsmen and falconers; for when they go forth to hunt they dwell sometimes for a whole month in the woods and mountains, wandering with their tents from place to place, taking their pleasure with their hounds and falcons, sleeping in the woods and fields in their tents, and carrying all that they need and all their provisions with them on camels and beasts of burden. You must know that all the princes, nobles, barons, knights, and citizens in Cyprus are the best and richest in the world, and now they dwell there with their children, but once they used to dwell on the mainland, in the cities of Syria and Judaea, and in the noble city of Acre; howbeit now that the mainland and its cities are lost they have fled to Cyprus, and abide there even to this day. There are also in Cyprus exceeding rich citizens and merchants, and no wonder, seeing that Cyprus is the furthest (east) of all Christian lands, wherefore all ships both great and small, and all merchandise of whatsoever kind and from whatsoever country, must needs come first

of all to Cyprus, and can in no wise pass by it. Moreover,
all pilgrims from all parts of the world whatsoever, when
bound for the parts beyond the sea, must needs come to
Cyprus, and every day from sunrise to sunset one hears
rumours and news there. In Cyprus also all the languages
of the world are heard and spoken, and are taught in
special schools ; and in Cyprus excellent wine grows on
lofty mountains exposed to the rays of the sun. This
wine is at first red, but after standing in an earthenware
jar for four, six, ten, or twenty years, it becomes white, and
all the while that it stands it does not lose strength, but
daily gains it, insomuch that usually nine parts of water
are added to one of wine ; and if a man were to drink a
whole cask of that wine, it would not make him drunk, but
would burn up and destroy his inside. Yet it is exceeding
wholesome to take some of the wine unmixed upon an
empty stomach, and nowhere are there better wine-
drinkers or more of them than in Cyprus. In Cyprus all
trees and herbs grow as they grow in the Holy Land.
Also in my time there were in Cyprus many nobles,
barons, and knights who had left Germany—to wit, the
Count of Vianden, the Count of Schwartzenberg, the Lord
of Sleyde, the Prince of Lichtenstein, and many others.
Also all the seaside places[1] in Turkey round about pay
tribute to the King of Cyprus—to wit, Candelor, Scalnun,
Sicki, and Satalia, and the other places and castles in their
neighbourhood. In this city of Satalia there are three

---

[1] 'Es ist wahrscheinlich, das unter diesen namen die städte
Kelenderis oder Kilindri, Selinus oder Selindri, Seleucia oder Selevke,
und Attalia, sämtlich an der küste klein Asiens in der nahe von
Cyperu zu verstehen sind. Vergl Sprüner's Atlas der Mittel Alters.'—
F. Deycks. With the help of Sprüner's invaluable atlas I have identi-
fied Candelor with Alaya Candelorum, Scalnun (possibly) with Selinus
(Trajanopolis) the modern Silintz, Sicki with Sequin, Siquinum (Syce),
and Satalia, of course, with Attalia, the modern Adalia.

heretical[1] races of men, and the city is divided by walls
and fosses into three parts: in the first dwell the Greeks,
who keep holy the Lord's day; in the second dwell the
Jews, who kept holy the Sabbath day; and in the third
dwell the Turks, who keep Friday holy. In the Greek
quarter there is a figure of the Blessed Virgin Mary painted
upon a tablet, of which tablets there are three in the
world—to wit, one at Rome, one at Constantinople, and
the third at Satalia; they are all of the same size, shape,
and appearance. It is believed that St. Luke painted
these three pictures from the Blessed Mary's own person,
and out of respect for this painting God works many
miracles there. It were too long to tell of the rest of the
riches and nobility of Cyprus.

XXIV.—THE CITIES BY THE SEA.

To return to my subject, one sails from Cyprus to some
one of the cities by the sea, in either Egypt or Syria.
These cities are as follows: Alexandria, Tripoli, Beyrout,
Byblium, Jaffa, Sidon, Tyre, Acre. Before going any
further I will say somewhat about these, that you may
know them. They all have been given different names to
those which they bore of old, after the Holy Land has
been lost and won so many times, and therefore I will say
a little about them, that you may know to whose lot these
cities fell when the Holy Land was won by the Christians.
You must know that none of these cities are more than a
day's journey distant from Cyprus. Now, Alexandria is
the first seaside city of Egypt, and one of the best of the
Soldan's cities. On one side it stands on the Nile, the
river of Paradise, which falls into the sea close by it, and its
other side is on the sea. This city is exceeding beauteous
and strong, and is fenced about with lofty towers and walls

[1] 'Perversa genera.' Compare Marco Polo, ed Panthier, p. 71.

which seem impregnable. It was once inhabited by the Christians, and is now by the Saracens, and within it is exceeding clean, being all whitewashed, and in the corner of every street it has a fountain of water running through pipes ; the city is carefully kept clean by watchmen, whose duty it is to see that no dirt be cast into the streets or fountains by anybody. In this city the Soldan keeps mercenary soldiers and his bodyguard, who guard the city and harbour. St. Mark the Evangelist was Patriarch in this city, and was martyred there, and in succession to him there still remains a Christian Patriarch there. In this city there still stands entire to this day a great and exceeding beauteous church, adorned in divers fashions with mosaic work and marble, wherein at the request of the Venetians Divine service is celebrated every day. Indeed, many other churches are still standing in Alexandria at this day, and in them rest the bodies of many saints. There are also many Christians and merchants living there. This city appears to the human eye to be impregnable, and yet it could be easily taken. I do not care to say any more about this matter. This city, which was of old called Alexandria, is now called Iscandria by its inhabitants. Near Alexandria is a place where St. Katharine was beheaded, and from whence she was borne by angels to Mount Sinai, a distance of about eighteen days' journey, and there are very many holy places and places of prayer in that city. Not far from Alexandria there is a village, all of whose inhabitants are Saracen workpeople, who weave mats wondrous well in divers fashions and with most curious skill. In this place or village stands a fair little church, wherein is a small grotto. In this grotto it is believed that St. John the Baptist was beheaded. The grotto is believed to have been a prison, and is known because of the position of the place, which is on the border of Egypt and Arabia. These same Saracen workpeople guard the grotto with the uttermost care and reverence, lighting it with lamps and candles, and each one of them according to his means pays some especial reverence to the church and grotto ; for they firmly believe and say that it has been proved by experience that if they did not hold the church in such great respect, and were to leave it unlighted for one night, rats would come forth from the ground and would pull to pieces and spoil all their matwork ; and they say that the more respect a man shows for the church and grotto aforesaid, the better he succeeds in his work. This place where the church now stands was of old called Metharonta in Arabic. The nearest city to Egypt is called Tripolis. It stands by the sea-shore at the foot of Mount Lebanon, and is a county which when the Holy Land was recovered by the Christians was given to the Count of Thoulouse. This land or county is fertile, and is famous for its grass, meadows, pastures, herbs, trees, and fruit beyond all other lands round about, and is exceeding beauteous ; wherefore beyond all other lands it is called a second paradise,[1] and has a loveliness beyond human comprehension. This land or county of gardens is traversed by a torrent which runs down from the loftiest mountain-peak of Lebanon with a frightful rush, so that its noise may be heard for more than a mile, and he who stands near it is made deaf for more than three days. Likewise there is a well of water which runs through this land or county, and rises therein ; it is a fountain ever welling forth from the flat ground, and never falling off in quantity or form, and is in all respects like the fountain in the city of Paderborn, which is called Padere. By these two streams, the fountain, and the well, the whole land is watered. These are the streams whereof

[1] Compare Fetellus, p. 47.

we read, ' A fountain of gardens, a well of living waters, and streams from Lebanon ' (Cant. iv. 15). And you must know that Mount Lebanon is exceeding long and in some places exceeding high. To my mind it is in all respects like the mount in these parts which is called Osning.[1] It extends from the beginning of the Promised Land as far as Cilicia, and is a mount full of the most delightful trees; fruits, and herbage that the heart of man can conceive. The mount is also filled with countless towns and villages, in all of which dwell Christians according to the Latin rite, who daily long for the coming of the Christians (on a Crusade), and many of whose bishops I have seen consecrated after the Latin rite. You must also know that the land up to which this mount reaches, which once was called Cilicia, is now called Lesser Armenia,[2] for the Armenians took that land from the Saracens by force, and have fought and quarrelled with them for five hundred years without interruption. In this land is the glorious city of Tarsus, wherein St. Paul the Apostle was born. But to return to my subject : there is another seaside city named Baruth, which is fairly well peopled, and which on the recovery of the Holy Land by the Christians fell to the lot of the Lord of Starkenberg. This city is mentioned by the Emperor (Justinian) in the Prologue[3] to the Digests, and formerly general studies greatly flourished here. In this city there stands a fair church dedicated to St. Nicholas, which is held in especial reverence by Christians. St. George converted this island to the faith of Christ, and

---

[1] The town of Paderborn, the source of the river Pader, and Mount Osning, which is in the Teutoburger Wald, point to Ludolph's home.

[2] See Anon., p. 15, note.

[3] The words are : ' Haec autem tria volumina a nobis composita tradi iis tam in regiis urbibus quam in Beryttensium pulcherrima civitate, quam et legum nutricem quis appellet, tantummodo volumus. —Dig., Proem., § 7 ; cf. §§ 9 and 10.

slew the dragon hard by it,[1] rescued the daughter of the King of the city from the dragon, and glorified the land with many miracles. The dragon's well may still be plainly seen. All pilgrims bound for Jerusalem meet together at this city and pass through it. Not far from this city there is another strong and well-fenced city named Byblium, which on the recovery of the Holy Land fell to the lot of the Knights of the Temple. One reads of this city in the Book of Kings[2]: *Porro Byblii portabant ligna.* This city, which was then called Byblium, is now called Ghiblet. Not far from this city there stands another city by the sea-shore named Japhe (Jaffa), which is still fairly well peopled. Once the common pilgrim-way passed through this city, but shortly before my time the Soldan laid waste the port out of fear of the King of France. This city has two other fair cities near it—to wit, Ramatha, wherein the prophet Samuel was born, and Ascalon. Jaffa is three days' journey from Jerusalem, or thereabouts, and is a county. The Count of Jaffa[3] is also Marshal of the Kingdom of Jerusalem and Lord of Ramatha and Ascalon, and so signs himself. In my time the Count of Japhe and Henry, Duke of Brunswick married two sisters. Not far from Jaffa is another exceeding beauteous seaside city, well fenced about with fine towers and walls, but utterly deserted. It is called Sidon, and

---

[1] Fabri, ii. 203.

[2] 1 Kings v. 18. 'Porro Giblii praeparaverunt ligna et lapides.' 'And Solomon's builders and Hiram's builders did hew them, and the stone-squarers; so they prepared timber and stones to build the house' (A.V.). See S.P.C.K. Bible, where we are told in a note that 'stone squarers' should read 'Giblites.' Cf. Poloner, p. 33, note.

[3] This must have been Hugh d'Ibelin, Count of Joppa and Ascalon, Seigneur of Rama, and Seneschal of Jerusalem in 1338, who married Isabelle d'Ibelin, widow of Ferdinand of Majorca. See 'Les Comtes de Jaffa et d'Ascalon' in 'Les Familles d'Outremer,' by M. Rey, Paris, 1869.

on the recovery of the Holy Land fell to the lot of a
knight called De Neapoli.[1] This city, which once was
called Sidon, is now called Sagette. Near this city is
another exceeding fair city, well fenced with fine towers
and walls, and standing strangely by itself on an isle in
the sea. It is named Tyre, but now it is almost deserted.
When the Holy Land was recovered, it fell to the lot of
Baldwin, Godfrey of Bouillon's brother. This city, which
once was called Tyre, is now called Sur. Between Tyre
and Sidon there stands a fair church at the place where
the Canaanitish woman called upon the Lord, as the
Gospel witnesseth, saying, ' Jesus departed thence into
the coasts of Tyre and Sidon, and behold, a Canaanitish
woman,' etc.[2]

XXV.—THE GLORIOUS CITY OF ACRE.

Near Tyre, at a distance of one day's journey along the
sea-shore, stands the glorious city of Acre, once the
thoroughfare of pilgrims and all other travellers, three
short days' journey from Jerusalem. Before going on to
anything else, I must say somewhat about this city of
Acre ; yet when I think of its present state I had liefer
weep than say anything. Whose heart is so hard that the
ruin and destruction of so great and noble a city would
not melt it ? This glorious city of Acre stands, as I have
said, on the sea-shore, built of squared hewn stones of more
than wonted size, with lofty and exceeding strong towers,
not a stone's-throw distant from one another all round the
walls. Each gate of the city stood between two towers,
and the walls were so great that two cars driving along
the top of them could easily pass one another, even as

---

[1] 'Eustach Grenier erhielt, A.D. 1111, Sidon zu Lehen.'—Wilken,
' Geschichten der Kreuzzuge.'

[2] Matt. xv. 21,

they are at the present day. On the other side also, toward the land, the city was fenced with notable walls and exceeding deep ditches, and variously equipped with divers outworks and defences, and conveniences for watchmen. The streets within the city were exceeding neat, all the walls of the houses being of the same height and all alike built of hewn stone, wondrously adorned with glass windows and paintings, while all the palaces and houses in the city were not built merely to meet the needs of those who dwelt therein, but to minister to human luxury and pleasure, each one as far as possible excelling the others in its glazing, painting, pavilions, and the other ornaments with which it was furnished within and beautified without.[1] The streets of the city were covered with silken cloths, or other fair awnings, to keep off the sun's rays. At every street corner there stood an exceeding strong tower, fenced with an iron door and iron chains. All the nobles dwelt in very strong castles and palaces along the outer edge of the city. In the midst of the city dwelt the mechanic citizens and merchants, each in his own especial street according to his trade, and all the dwellers in the city, like the Normans of old, held themselves to be noble, and bore themselves like nobles, as of a truth they were.[2] First

[1] This entire account of Ptolemais before its capture is repeated word for word in the Latin chronicle of the Dominican monk, Hermann Cornerus, of Lubeck, written A.D. 1435. See Eccard's 'Corpus Historiarum Medii Aevi,' vol. ii., p. 941.—F. Deycks.

[2] Compare the following extract from Villani's 'History of Florence,' book vii., chap. cxliv. Muratori, 'Scriptores Rerum Italicarum,' tom. xiii., pp. 337, 338. 'Egli è vera cosa, che perchè i Sarracini haveano ne tempi dinanzi tolte a' Christiani la Città di Antiochia, et quella di Tripoli, e quella di Suri, & piu altre Città, che i Christiani teneano alla marina, la Città d' Acri era molto cresciuta di gente, & di podere, però che altra terra non si tenea per li Christiani in Soria, sì che per lo Re di Gierusalem, & per quello di Cipri, e'l Prenze d' Antiochia, & quello di Suri, & di Tripoli, & la Magione del Tempio,

there dwelt therein the King of Jerusalem and his brethren, and very many nobles of the family ; the princes of Galilee, the princes of Antioch and the chief captain of the King of France, the Duke of Caesarea, the Lord of Sur[1] and the Lord of Tiberias, the Lord of Sagette,[2] the Count of Tripoli, the Count of Jaffa, the Lord of Beyrout, the Lord of Ibelin,[3] the Lord of Pysan,[4] the Lord of Arsuf,[5] the Lord of Vaus,[6] and the nobles of Blanchegarde. All these princes, dukes, counts, nobles, and barons walked about the streets in royal state, with golden coronets on their heads, each of them like a king, with his knights, his followers, his mercenaries, and his retainers, his clothing and his war-horse wondrously bedecked with gold and silver, all vying one with another in beauty and novelty of device, and each man apparelling himself with the most thoughtful care. Every day they practised themselves in joustings, games, tournaments, and every sort of military display,[7] and each one had his own liberty or privileged piece of ground[8]

& dello Spedale, & l' altre Magioni & Legato del Papo, & quelli, ch' erano oltra mare per lo Re di Francia, & per lo Re d' Inghilterra, tutti faceano capo in Acri, & haveano 17 signorie di sangue, la quale era una grande confusione.' Villani died 1348.

[1] Tyre.

[2] So spelt in Dr. F. Deycks's text. The place which the Crusaders called Sagitta, or Sajette, is the ancient Sidon, now Sayda.

[3] 'The fortress of Ibelin, about ten miles from Ascalon, was built on the traditional site of Gath in 1144.' See 'The City of Herod and Saladin,' p. 296.

[4] Al. Poysan. Probably Bethshan. See 'Names and Places in the Old and New Testament,' by G. Armstrong. A. Watt, London, 1889.

[5] Antipatris, between Jaffa and Caesarea. Cf. 'The Condition of City of Jerusalem,' p. 32, notes 2, 4. See also C. R. Conder in the 'Survey of Western Palestine,' vol. v., p. 252. The Crusaders mistakenly identified it with Ashdod. Sprüner, 'Atlas der Mittelaelters,' has Arsuf, Arsur, Assur, Antipatrida.

[6] See preface.

[7] *Deductio.*

[8] Compare Fabri, vol. ii., p. 376.

beside his own palace or castle. Therein also dwelt, to fight against the Saracens for the Catholic faith, the Master and brethren of the Knights Templars, armed knights; the Master and brethren of the Order of St. John of Jerusalem, armed knights; and the Master and brethren of the house of the Teutonic Order, armed knights; likewise the Master and brethren of the Order of St. Thomas[1] of Canterbury, armed knights; and the Master and brethren of the Order of St. Lazarus, armed knights. All these dwelt in Acre, and had the headquarters of their Order there, and they and their fellows fought day and night against the Saracens. There also dwelt in Acre the richest merchants under heaven, who were gathered together therein out of all nations; there were Pisans, Genoese, and Lombards, by whose accursed quarrels the city was lost, for they also bore themselves like nobles. There dwelt therein also exceeding rich merchants of other nations, for from sunrise to sunset all parts of the world brought merchandise thither, and everything that can be found in the world that is wondrous or strange used to be brought thither because of the nobles and princes who dwelt there. It would take long to tell of the other glories, wonders, and beauties of Acre one by one,

[1] 'Another little-known Order merits notice. An English priest, William, chaplain to Ralph de Diceto, devoted himself to burying the Christian dead at Acre. Afterwards he built a chapel and bought ground for a cemetery, which he dedicated to St. Thomas the Martyr. Through the patronage of Becket's sister, a hospital of St. Thomas the Martyr of Canterbury at Acre was built in London on the site of the Archbishop's house; and in 1231, when Peter des Roches was in Palestine, he established these knights under the rule of the Templars. These knights of St. Thomas of Acre wore their own mantle with a cross of red and white, and have the distinction of being one of the few peculiarly English Orders. They survived in the kingdom of Cyprus till near the close of the fourteenth century.' 'The Crusades': 'Story of the Nations,' T. F. Unwin, 1894. See also Stubbs's 'Lectures on Mediaeval History,' pp. 182-185.

neither could any man tell fully of them all. This is that renowned city of Acre, which once was called Ptolemais, wherein Judas (?) Maccabeus was treacherously slain by Tryphon, as is told in the Book of Maccabees. Likewise, this is that city of Acre[1] wherein was the idol Beelzebub, what time Ahaziah, King of Israel, fell down through a lattice in his upper chamber that was in Samaria, and said unto his servants, ' Go, inquire of Baal-zebub, the god of Ekron, whether I shall recover of this disease,' as is told at length in the Book of Kings.[2]

XXVI.—THE LOSS OF THE CITY OF ACRE.

After having told of the glories and beauties of Acre, I will now shortly tell you of its fall and ruin, and the cause of its loss, even as I heard the tale told by right truthful men, who well remembered it. While, then, the grand doings of which I have spoken were going on in Acre, at the instigation of the devil there arose a violent and hateful quarrel in Lombardy between the Guelfs and the Ghibellines, which brought all evil upon the Christians. Those Lombards who dwelt in Acre took sides in this same quarrel, especially the Pisans and Genoese, both of whom had an exceeding strong party in Acre. These men made treaties and truces with the Saracens, to the end that they might the better fight against one another within the city. When Pope Urban[3] heard of this, he grieved for Christendom and for the Holy Land, and sent twelve thousand mercenary troops across the sea to help the Holy Land

[1] Like most mediæval writers, Ludolph confuses Acre (Acon) with Accaron (O.T., Ekron). See Anon. II., chap. i., note.

[2] 2 Kings i. 2.

[3] Urban IV. reigned 1261-1264 ; it cannot therefore be he, but Jerome d'Ascoli, Nicholas IV., 1288-1292, who is meant.

and Christendom. When these men came across the sea to Acre they did no good, but abode by day and by night in taverns and places of ill-repute, took and plundered merchants and pilgrims in the public streets, broke the treaty, and did much evil. Melot Sapheraph, Soldan of Babylon,[1] an exceeding wise man, most potent in arms and bold in action, when he heard of this, and knew of the hateful quarrels of the people of Acre, called together his counsellors and held a parliament in Babylon, wherein he complained that the truces had frequently been broken and violated, to the prejudice of himself and his people. After a debate had been held upon this matter, he gathered together a mighty host, and reached the city of Acre without any resistance, because of their quarrels with one another, cutting down and wasting all the vineyards and fruit-trees and all the gardens and orchards, which are most lovely thereabout. When the Master of the Templars, a very wise and brave knight, saw this, he feared that the fall of the city was at hand, because of the quarrels of the citizens. He took counsel with his brethren about how peace could be restored, and then went out to meet the Soldan, who was his own very especial friend, to ask him whether they could by any means repair the broken truce. He obtained these terms from the Soldan, to wit, that because of his love for the Soldan and the honour in which the Soldan held him, the broken truce might be restored by every man in Acre paying one Venetian penny. So the Master of the Templars was glad, and, departing from the Soldan, called together all the people and preached a sermon to them in the Church of St. Cross, setting forth how, by his prayers, he had prevailed upon the Soldan to grant that the broken treaty might be restored by a payment of one Venetian penny by each man, that therewith

[1] Gino.

everything might be settled and quieted. He advised them by all means so to do, declaring that the quarrels of the citizens might bring a worse evil upon the city than this—as indeed they did. But when the people heard this, they cried out with one voice that he was the betrayer of the city, and was guilty of death. The Master, when he heard this, left the church, hardly escaped alive from the hands of the people, and took back their answer to the Soldan. When the Soldan heard this, knowing that, owing to the quarrels of the people, none of them would make any resistance, he pitched his tents, set up sixty machines, dug many mines beneath the city walls, and for forty days and nights, without any respite, assailed the city with fire, stones, and arrows, so that (the air) seemed to be stiff with arrows. I have heard a very honourable knight say that a lance which he was about to hurl from a tower among the Saracens was all notched with arrows before it left his hand. There were at that time in the Soldan's army six hundred thousand[1] armed men, divided into three companies ; so one hundred thousand continually besieged the city, and when they were weary another hundred thousand took their place before the same, two hundred thousand stood before the gates of the city ready for battle, and the duty of the remaining two hundred thousand was to supply them with everything that they needed. The gates were never closed, nor was there an hour of the day without some hard fight being fought against the Saracens by the Templars or other brethren dwelling therein. But the numbers of the Saracens grew so fast that after one hundred thousand of them had been slain two hundred

---

[1] With regard to these outrageous figures, and the mythical complexion of the whole story, compare Wilken's ' Geschichte der Kreuzzuge,' vii. 757, and Dr. F. Deycks's work, ' Über altere Pilgerfahrten,' p. 49.

thousand came back. Yet, even against all this host, they would not have lost the city had they but helped one another faithfully ; but when they were fighting without the city, one party would run away and leave the other to be slain, while within the city one party would not defend the castle or palace belonging to the other,[1] but purposely let the other party's castles, palaces, and strong places be stormed and taken by the enemy, and each one knew and believed his own castle and place to be so strong that he cared not for any other's castle or strong place. During this confusion the Masters and brethren of the Orders alone defended themselves, and fought unceasingly against the Saracens, until they were nearly all slain ; indeed, the Master and brethren of the house of the Teutonic Order, together with their followers and friends, all fell dead at one and the same time. As this went on with many battles and many thousands slain on either side, at last the fulfilment of their sins and the time of the fall of the city drew near ; when the fortieth day of its siege was come, in the year of our Lord one thousand two hundred and ninety-two, on the twelfth day of the month of May, the most noble and glorious city of Acre, the flower, chief and pride of all the cities of the East, was taken. The people of the other cities, to wit, Jaffa, Tyre, Sidon and Ascalon, when they heard this, left all their property behind and fled to Cyprus. When first the Saracens took Acre they got in through a breach in the wall near the King of Jerusalem's castle, and when they were among the people of the city within, one party still would not help the other, but each defended his own castle and palace, and the Saracens had a much longer siege, and fought at much less advantage when they were within the city than when they were without, for it was wondrously fortified. Indeed,

---

[1] *Altius = alterius.*

we read in the stories of the loss of Acre that because of the sins of the people thereof the four elements[1] fought on the side of the Saracens. First the air became so thick, dark, and cloudy that, while one castle, palace, or strong place was being stormed or burned, men could hardly see in the other castles and palaces, until their castles and palaces were attacked, and then for the first time they would have willingly defended themselves, could they have come together. Fire fought against the city, for it consumed it. Earth fought against the city, for it drank up its blood. Water also fought against the city, for it being the month of May, wherein the sea is wont to be very calm, when the people of Acre plainly saw that because of their sins and the darkening of the air they could not see their enemies, they fled to the sea, desiring to sail to Cyprus, and whereas at first there was no wind at all at sea, of a sudden so great a storm arose that no other ship, either great or small, could come near the shore, and many who essayed to swim off to the ships were drowned. Howbeit, more than one hundred thousand men escaped to Cyprus. I have heard from a most honourable lord, and from other truthful men who were present, that more than five hundred most noble ladies and maidens, the daughters of kings and princes, came down to the seashore, when the city was about to fall, carrying with them all their jewels and ornaments of gold and precious stones, of priceless value, in their bosoms, and cried aloud, asking whether there were any sailor there who would take all their jewels, and take whichever of them he chose to wife, if only he would take them, even naked, to some safe land or island. A sailor received them all into his ship, took them across to Cyprus, with all their goods, for nothing, and went his way. But who he was, whence he came, or

[1] Marino Sanuto book iii., part xii., chap. xxi., ad finem.

whither he went, no man knows to this day.[1] Very many
other noble ladies and damsels were drowned or slain. It
would take long to tell what great grief and anguish was
there. While the Saracens were within the city, but before
they had taken it, fighting from castle to castle, from one
palace and strong place to another, so many men perished on
either side that they walked over their corpses as it were
over a bridge. When all the inner city was lost, all who still
remained alive fled into the exceeding strong castle of the
Templars, which was straightway invested on all sides by
the Saracens ; yet the Christians bravely defended it for
two months, and before it almost all the nobles and chiefs
of the Soldan's army fell dead. For when the city inside
the walls was burned, yet the towers of the city, and the
Templars' castle, which was in the city, remained, and
with these the people of the city kept the Saracens within
the city from getting out, as before they had hindered their
coming in, until of all the Saracens who had entered the
city not one remained alive, but all fell by fire or by the
sword. When the Saracen nobles saw the others lying
dead, and themselves unable to escape from the city, they
fled for refuge into the mines which they had dug under
the great tower, that they might make their way through
the wall and so get out. But the Templars and others
who were in the castle, seeing that they could not hurt the
Saracens with stones and the like, because of the mines
wherein they were, undermined the great tower of the
castle, and flung it down upon the mines and the Saracens
therein, and all perished alike. When the other Saracens
without the city saw that they had thus, as it were, failed
utterly, they treacherously made a truce with the Templars

[1] This story is repeated by Lampadius in his ' Mellificium Historicum,' A.D. 1617, part iii., p. 312. Cf. Fuller's ' Holy Warre,'
book iv., chap. xxxiii.

and Christians on the condition that they should yield up
the castle, taking all their goods with them, and should
destroy it, but should rebuild the city on certain terms, and
dwell therein in peace as heretofore. The Templars and
Christians, believing this, gave up the castle and marched
out of it, and came down from the city towers. When the
Saracens had by this means got possession both of the
castle and of the city towers, they slew all the Christians
alike, and led away the captives to Babylon. Thus Acre
has remained empty and deserted even to this day. In
Acre and the other places nearly a hundred and six thousand men were slain or taken, and more than two hundred
thousand escaped from thence. Of the Saracens more
than three hundred thousand were slain, as is well known
even to this day. The Saracens spent forty days over the
siege of the city, fifty days within the city before it was
taken, and two months over the siege of the Templars'
castle. When the glorious city of Acre thus fell, all the
Eastern people sung of its fall in hymns of lamentation,
such as they are wont to sing over the tombs of their dead,
bewailing the beauty, the grandeur, and the glory of Acre
even to this day. Since that day all Christian women,
whether gentle or simple, who dwell along the eastern shore
(of the Mediterranean) dress in black garments of mourning
and woe for the lost grandeur of Acre, even to this day.

After this the Saracens worked for many years en-
deavouring to utterly subvert and destroy down to their
foundations all the walls, towers, castles, and palaces, lest
the Christians should rebuild them; yet in hardly any
place have they been able to beat them down to the height
of a man, but all the churches, walls, and towers, and very
many castles and palaces, remain almost entire, and, if it
pleased God, could with great care be restored throughout
to their former state. At this day about sixty Saracen

mercenaries dwell in Acre as a garrison for the city and port, and make a living out of silk and birds, for there are so many partridges and pigeons to be found in Acre, that all the birds to be seen in this country are not to be compared to them. These mercenaries have an especial delight in Germans, whom they straightway recognise by their appearance and walk, and drink wine deeply with them, albeit it is forbidden by their law. Thus have I told how the glorious city of Acre was lost by quarrels, and from that time forth all the glory of the Holy Land, of its kings, princes, and other lords, has been carried over into Cyprus, as you have already heard.

XXVII.—OF GAZA AND AZOTUS.

But to return to my subject : from Acre one goes on to Gaza, once an exceeding fine city of the Philistines, now almost a desert, whose iron gates Samson broke and took away with him into a mountain. The distance from Acre to Gaza is twenty-three miles, and on the way one sees the following places. But before going further, I propose to tell you somewhat about the cities of the Philistines. Round about this city of Gaza lies the land of Palestine, wherein we see that four exceeding great cities once stood, which now have been brought down to small villages, all save two—to wit, Azotus (Ashdod) and Gath. You must know that the land which once was called Philistia is now called Palestine, and that the city which once was called Azotus is now called Arsuf,[1] whose noble lord I have often seen. And the city which once was called Gath[2] is now

[1] Arsuf=Antipatris. Balian d'Ibelin was Seigneur d'Arsuf in 1368.

[2] 'Scandalium, south-west from Tyre, built by Alexander the Great, is not the same as Gath,' says F. Deycks, who identifies the Scandalium of the Crusaders with Alexandroscene, the place where Alexander's tent was pitched during the siege of Tyre. See Theoderich, chap. li., and Tobler's note thereto.

called Scandalium, a name which Baldwin, King of
Jerusalem, gave it when he was building it. It was in
this city that Goliath was born, whom David slew, and
many other wonders may be read of about this city. From
this city onwards all the cities and villages, castles and
places, on the sea-shore aforesaid, and for a space of four
miles inland, have been laid waste and remain so to this
day. For as soon as the Holy Land, Syria, and Acre
were lost, the Saracens thought that they should possess in
peace all the aforesaid places, cities, villages, and castles
on the sea-shore. But at that time the people of Gath, or
Scandalium, were exceeding strong men, and very valiant
in arms; indeed, it is said that the place is of such a
nature that men born there are fiercer than other men.
These same people of Gath, albeit few in number, being
less than one thousand, are noble and valiant, and know
all the roads and by-ways of the land; for they are wont
to wander hither and thither with arms in their hands,
serving for hire, and they know the manners and customs
of the Saracens, and the going in and the coming out of
the land, and they never rested, but went to and fro continually, by land and by water, by night and by day,
dressed in Saracen clothing, with arms concealed beneath
it. While they were among the Saracens, they went as
Saracen merchants,[1] and entered with them into their
cities and villages, ate and drank with them, and by
degrees gathered together; and whenever they thought
that they had a good opportunity, they took and burned
the town or village in which they happened to be, and
slew the Saracens or sold them for slaves. When the
Saracens saw that they could not guard themselves against

---

[1] I hardly know whether this is to be taken as serious history. A
story of the same sort is told by William of Tyre about the rescue of
Baldwin II. from Khortbert.

these men, they deserted their cities and villages and went away, yet seldom escaped, and thus all the places along the sea-shore, the cities and villages and other places as far as four miles inland, were made utterly desolate even to this day. I have heard from truthful men who were present when these things came to pass, and the public talk and rumour of them still remains there, that so great fear fell upon the Saracens because of these aforesaid men of Gath, that as far as six days' journey therefrom mothers used to quiet their crying children with this word Scandalium. Moreover, no man dared meet another on the road, for because of the people of Scandalium no precaution would make a man fully safe. But to return to my subject : near Acre there is a river of no great size named Belen.[1] This river rolls down a sort of glassy sand, which is carried away to distant lands. There is likewise another river near Acre, on one side of which no serpent or venomous thing can live, though they can do so well on the other side ; and it has been proved that serpents cast across this river die straightway.

XXVIII.—OF MOUNT CARMEL.

Also near Acre, on the right hand, three miles away, not far from the sea, stands Mount Carmel, which is smooth, and wide, and most beauteous at the top, adorned with much grass and pleasant places. On this mount dwelt Elijah the prophet, and wrought many miracles. On this mount also, at Elijah's word, the captains of fifty of Ahaziah, King of Israel, were consumed by fire from heaven. On this mount also Elijah prayed that it might not rain upon the earth, and it did not rain for three years

---

[1] ' This is the Belus whose glass manufactures are mentioned by Pliny and Tacitus.'—Dr. F. Deycks.

and six months, as we read in the Book of Kings. On this mount it may be seen that there once stood an exceeding fine convent built in honour of St. Mary, and the friars who derive their origin from thence are called Carmelites to this day. They are begging friars, and one may see that they once had fifteen fair convents in the Holy Land. On one side of the mount there is a clear fountain running into the sea, from which Elijah the prophet used to drink, and it is called Elijah's Fountain to this day. At another place at the foot of the mount one may see where there stood a city of the Templars, now utterly destroyed, called Cyphas.[1] Not very far from this city there is a small fountain, which is one of the sources of the Jordan. At the end of Mount Carmel there was once a fair city, now destroyed, named Jezreel, where Jezebel took away Naboth's vineyard, and was cast down at the same place, as we read in the Book of Kings.[2] Near this city are the plains of Megiddo, wherein Josiah, King of Judah, was slain. Not far from Mount Carmel, on the left-hand side, there once stood a fair city, now destroyed, named Sepphora, which stood on a hill, and wherein St. Anne, the Blessed Mary's mother, was born.

After passing over Mount Carmel one crosses a river, which is one of the sources of the Jordan, and comes to Caesarea of Palestine, which once was called Dor, and now is called Caesarea of Palestine, but is utterly destroyed. In this city there was a fair church made out of the house of Cornelius,[3] whom Peter converted to the true faith. This same city, on the recovery of the Holy Land, came into the possession of a certain knight of these parts,

[1] Haifa.

[2] 1 Kings xxi.

[3] Compare the Bordeaux Pilgrim, p. 17 : 'Qualiter Sita est Urbs Sancta Jerusalem,' 32.

named De Horne, whose son-in-law's widow was living even in my own time, for I have often seen her and talked upon this subject with her. Going on from Caesarea, one comes to what once was a fair city, but now is deserted, called Pilgrim's Castle, which of old was called Assur.[1] This city was given to the Templars by Godfrey de Bouillon, the first Christian King of Jerusalem, for a memorial of himself. Going on from Assur, or Pilgrims' Castle, one comes to a very fair city, tolerably full of people even at this day, called Ascalon. Going on from Ascalon, one comes to Joppa, an exceeding ancient and beauteous city standing on the sea-shore. It was the port of this city that the prophet Jonah entered when he essayed to flee from before the face of the Lord. It is about two days' journey distant from Jerusalem, but pilgrims are not able to land at the port. Inland, not far from Joppa, there stands a fair city, once called Ruma,[2] but now called Bael, situated in a most beauteous, pleasant, and delectable place, and inhabited by Christians alone. It is believed that no Jew or Saracen could live or dwell therein for more than a year. All the wine drunk by the Christians in Jerusalem and the other places is brought from hence. On the left hand side of this Ruma, or Bael, there stands a fair city, still well peopled, called Diospolis, or by another name, Lydda. In this city the glorious martyr St. George suffered martyrdom, and was beheaded. There is an exceeding fair church, well adorned with mosaic work and marble, wherein, in the choir, the place of his beheading is publicly shown. After seeing all these things one comes first to Gaza, whereof I said somewhat already, because I told

---

[1] Castrum Peregrinorum, also called Petra Incisa. See 'Guidebook,' p. 34. Assur is not Castrum Peregrinorum, but Athlit, which was fortified by the Templars, and lost by them after the fall of Acre in 1291. See also 'La Citez de Jherusalem,' p. 31, note, and preface.

[2] 'Ruina' in two MSS.; Ramla, the N.T. Arimathaea.

5

you of the other cities of the Philistines. It is four days' journey from Acre to Gaza, visiting all the places aforesaid. Going on from Gaza, one comes to a castle called Dar in Arabic, which is the last place in Syria as you go down into Egypt. Going this way, one leaves Jerusalem on the left hand, twenty miles off, or thereabouts. These are not the common pilgrim ways, but are good ones for seeing first Arabia and Egypt, and all that therein is. From the castle of Dar one goes to Egypt across the sandy desert in seven days. In this desert there is no lack of anything needful save only water, which can be well carried in skins on camels. Good Saracen inns may be found at the end of each day's journey, and all that one needs except wine.

XXIX.—OF EGYPT.

After crossing this desert one comes into Egypt, on entering which one finds places of the greatest beauty and delight, full of all good things that the heart of man can conceive, and full of everything needful except wine. Travelling onward toward New Babylon[1] one comes to a very beautiful and delightful village called Bélyab, and so, leaving Alexandria and Damietta on the sea-shore, one goes along the highroad and comes to Carra (Cairo) and New Babylon, which are two exceeding great cities not far apart, standing on the Nile, the river of Paradise. The city which once was called Carra (Cairo) is now called Alcayre. In this city of old dwelt Pharaoh when he persecuted the Hebrews. Herein also signs and wonders

---

[1] 'New Babylon was a fortress, built by Babylonian exiles over against Memphis in the time of the Persian kings' (Strabo, xvii. 1).—Dr. F. Deycks. But most mediaeval writers call Cairo 'Babylon' without any reservation.

were wrought by Moses and Aaron, as the Bible testifies. Near Carra (Cairo) on a mount, not high, but rocky, stands the Soldan's palace, and there are very many other strange and wondrous things. Above all, in these two cities one sees elephants and gryphons. You must know that Cairo is bigger than Babylon, and is not two cross-bow-shots distant from it; for Babylon stands on the bank of the Nile, but Cairo stands a little way off the Nile. Now, Cairo is bigger than Babylon, for I have heard from merchants that they reckoned Cairo to be seven times as big as Paris. In Cairo there are low buildings like ovens; in them are furnaces, wherein eggs are laid upon dung, and by this heat chickens are hatched and come forth from the eggs. The master then takes them and gives them to an old woman, who nurses and cherishes the chickens in her bosom, even as a hen does beneath its wings, and feeds them and takes care of them. There are numberless old women in those parts who have no means of livelihood save by nursing and taking care of chickens, wherefore the fowls there are like the sands of the sea for number. A countryman often drives five or six thousand fowls to market once a week, even as a shepherd drives his sheep, and he takes a camel or some other beast with panniers, which he fills with the eggs laid by the fowls on the way, and when he comes into the market set apart for fowls, he never loses one single fowl, neither do one man's fowls ever mix themselves with another's, which is indeed wonderful, when so many thousand fowls all meet together in one place. Moreover, near Babylon there is an exceeding fertile place with very rich pasture, called Goshen, where the patriarch Jacob dwelt at the instance of Joseph in Pharaoh's time, as the Bible tells us.

XXX.—Of the Garden of Balsam.[1]

Moreover, near Cairo, on the side toward the Syrian desert, is the Garden of Balsam, which is half a stone's-throw across, and not very strongly walled or fenced about. In this garden there are five wells, which water the shoots and shrubs of balsam, and each shoot or shrub has its own especial guardian, who cleanses it, dresses it, and washes it as carefully as he does his own body. These shoots or shrubs of balsam do not grow so high as two ells, and have a threefold leaf. At the beginning of March, when the time of its ripening is at hand, it is watched yet more carefully, and when it is ripe the shoots and shrubs are cut and wounded, like as vines are pruned, and their wounds and cuts are bound up with muslin. From these wounded shoots the balsam drips out, as water does from a cut vine, and oozes into the muslin bound round the wound. Beneath each wounded branch and bandage there hangs a silver cup, into which the best balsam drops.[2]

Thus the tree is cut when the balsam runs; at that time the Soldan of Babylon is very busy, being himself present in the garden, and so carefully does he guard it that no one but he himself can obtain a drop of balsam by any means. But when the legates and ambassadors of certain kings and princes come from foreign parts, he gives each of them a

[1] This account of the Garden of Balsam is word for word the same as that of John of Hildesheim in his ' History of the Three Kings.' With regard to the properties attributed to balsam, the curious reader may compare H. Crombach's account of myrrh in ' Primitiae Gentium, sive Historia S.S. Trium Magorum,' tom. ii., chap. xli.

[2] The Berlin MS. Diez C., marked ' A ' by Dr. Deycks, has here the words, ' As may be seen in the figure of this tree,' and a coloured picture of the balsam-tree, which has three large and three small boughs, from each ot which hangs a silver cup with a red spot in the middle.

little glass phial, made specially for this purpose, with balsam therein, which he thinks to be the richest jewel that he could give. Afterwards, when all the (true and good) balsam has thus oozed out, the guardians of the shrubs cut off the ends of the shoots, which belong to them, boil them in water, and then whatever balsam was left in the tops of the shoots boils out like fat, and swims upon the top of the water like oil, whence it is taken up with a spoon, put into a vessel, and left to stand for some time. Even this balsam is of great value, albeit it has been boiled, and it is of a reddish colour, with some mixture of black; but the crude balsam which drips forth naturally is of the colour of wine.[1] And you must know that crude balsam is the most precious jewel in the world, wherefore the holy patriarchs were wont to mix it with holy oil for anointing, and whatsoever flesh is touched with crude balsam never rots or corrupts, and when it is dripping fresh from the tree, if a drop be placed in a man's hand, it will drip through on the other side and pass through his hand. Moreover, if four or five drops of crude balsam be put into a man's eyes, which are going blind through lack of moisture, old age, or any other infirmity, straightway his eyes will for ever remain exactly as they were at the instant when the balsam was poured in, getting neither better nor worse; wherefore, in one way it is a perilous venture to try, unless a man altogether despairs of his sight. This fact is clearly shown in many corpses of great men of old which have been found entirely uncorrupt, because they have been anointed with balsam. Likewise, if the scar of a new wound, when it is beginning to heal, be rubbed round once a day with half a drop of balsam on a pencil, it straightway restores the skin of the wound as it was before, and makes no blemish, and no one can see that there ever

[1] See Sir John Maundeville, chap. v.

was a scar in the place. Moreover, this boiled balsam is an exceeding noble drug, and is very good for the scars of wounds, as aforesaid ; it is especially good when a man falls down from a high place, for then if he takes some of it his whole body, which was broken inside, would be restored and made whole again. It has also much power over the eyes, and is good for anointing flesh meat that it may not decay. But in all and every way it has less power than crude balsam ; for it is forced out by boiling, whereas the crude balsam oozes out naturally. You must know that only Christian men are able to tend and keep the Garden of Balsam, for if other men were to tend and keep it they would straightway shrivel up and die, as hath often been proved. The Blessed Virgin Mary[1] dwelt with the Boy Jesus in the place where the Garden of Balsam now is, when she fled into Egypt from before the face of Herod ; and she constantly washed her sheets and clothes and Jesus in the fountains which water the garden, for which cause it is thought of a truth that the balsam grows here, for as far as we know it is found nowhere else in all the world.[2] It would take long to tell of the other virtues and glories of balsam, neither can I recall them to my mind. In my time, among the Christian guardians, there were four Germans, one from Schwartzenburg, who once had been a

[1] Fabri, vol. iii., p. 2 (part ii., p. 746), came to the village of Busiris, where his dragoman took the party into the castle of the village, wherein are the Lord Soldan's hot baths, and summer palace, near the Fountain of the Sun, which is the Fountain of the Blessed Virgin, adjoining which is the Garden of Balsam. The pilgrims' lodging had windows overlooking the garden, which he describes at length.

[2] Fabri declares that the Queen of Sheba brought balsam to Solomon, who planted it in the vineyard of Engaddi : ' Botrus cypri in vinea Engaddi,' Cant. i. 14. ' Cyprus,' which the A.V. translates ' camphire,' seems to have been thought in the Middle Ages to refer to the island. Consequently a ' vineyard of Engaddi ' was established there by the Crusaders.

renegade, and one other, a one-eyed man named Nicholas, who was a very good man, as the Christian captives bore witness. He was taken captive at Acre, but the Soldan set him free because of his goodness, and made him guard the steps of his bedchamber,

XXXI.—The Christians and the Ancient Tombs.

You must know that in Babylon and Cairo, in my time, there were about four thousand Christian captives, not counting children. These men have there a Patriarch, priests, churches, and very many venerable relics of the saints; above all, they have the entire body of St. Barbara[1] the virgin, for which in my time many kings and princes begged, but out of consideration for the comfort of the captive Christians the Soldan never so much as cut off one limb from her body. The Christian captives there merrily keep St. Barbara's Eve,[2] just as in these parts people keep St. Martin's Eve, sending to one another the seeds of divers plants. Near New Babylon, on the other side of the Nile, toward the Egyptian desert, stand many tombs of wondrous size, and one of great beauty, built of great squared stones. Among these are two exceeding great square sepulchres, once of great beauty. On one of them there are many inscriptions carved, in Latin on one wall, in Greek on another, in Hebrew on the third, and in Chaldean and many unknown tongues on the fourth. On the first wall, where the writings are in Latin, these verses

[1] 'Item alia ecclesia beatæ Barbaræ virginis, qua corpus ipsius in parvo monumento marmoreo conservatur.'—Wilhelm von Boldinsel, chap. iii.. Fabri somewhere remarks that he had seen so many relics of St. Barbara that he thought that there must have been more than one saint of that name.

[2] See John of Hildesheim's 'Historia trium Regum,' p. 154, in the Early English Text Society's edition, by C. Horstmann; Trübner, 1886. Also p. 280 in the Latin version at the end.

are carved, as far as they can be read, because of their age,
as follows :

> ' Vidi pyramidas sine te, dulcissime frater,
> Et tibi quod potui lacrimas hic moesta profudi.
> Et nostri memorem luctus hanc sculpo querelam—
> S(c)it nomen Decimi Anni pyramidis alta,
> Pontificis, comitisque tuis, 'Trajane, triumphis
> Lustra sex intra censoris consulis esse.'[1]

> *Alone, alas ! the Pyramids I see,*
> *And can but weep, my brother dear, for thee.*
> *Upon the stone I've sadly carved thy name,*
> *The greatest Pyramid now knows the fame*
> *Of Annius Decimus, who fought for Rome*
> *With Trajan, and returned in triumph home,*
> *Who, e'en before his thirtieth birthday passed,*
> *Was Pontiff, Consul, Censor, too, at last.'*

The interpretation of these verses I leave to the discreet
reader's judgment. These tombs are called by the natives
Pharaoh's granaries,[2] and very many other wonders are to
be seen in and near Babylon. As I have heard from many
truthful men and merchants, ancient Babylon, where the
tower of Babel was, is some thirty days' journey distant
from this Babylon, to the north-east, in Chaldaea, near
Baldach. And you must know that, after having diligently for a space of five years conversed by day and by
night with all men who could speak any human language,
and after making daily inquiries of divers people, from all
of whom I got some information, I was nevertheless never
able to make out from any living creature any more about
ancient Babylon, where the tower Babel was, than here
follows.

[1] These verses are quoted, with slight variations, by W. von Boldinsel, who reads 'Cetianni' in line 4, whence Dr. C. L. Grotefend, his
editor, conjectures that the person alluded to may have been D. Titianus,
who was Consul A.D. 127. Fabri says, ii. 89 *b* (vol. iii., p. 43), that he
saw these verses, and gives an almost identical version of them.

[2] Fabri, vol. iii., p. 67 ; 'Speculum Historiale,' book v., chap. i.

XXXII.—Ancient Babylon, or Baldach.

In Eastern Chaldaea there is an exceeding fair and noble city, powerful beyond measure, and at this day one of the best of all the cities of the East, named Baldach.[1] It stands on the banks of the Euphrates, one of the rivers of Paradise, and they who dwell there say and believe that half a mile or thereabouts from it stood ancient Babylon. This also is proved by the vast ruins and immense piles of buildings of divers sorts, and of stones, which have a strange aspect from a distance, especially at the place where the tower of Babel stood, where the confusion of tongues arose. Another proof lies in the impassable road between the ruins and Baldach, by reason of the venomous creatures; and many other signs show that ancient Babylon stood there, as the inhabitants do most firmly believe : for because of those venomous creatures ancient Babylon was removed, and called by another name, to wit, Baldach. I can tell nothing else that is true concerning old Babylon, nor could I ever learn anything more about it from anyone in those parts. In this city of Baldach there are now the richest and best merchants under heaven, neither is there in any place in the East so much and so many different kinds of merchandise as there. In this city used to dwell the Caliph, that is, the successor of Mahomet, to whom the Saracens render obedience in all things, even as do the Christians to the Pope, the successor of St. Peter. I will tell you somewhat about the loss of this city of Baldach,

[1] 'Dr. Rock ("Textile Fabrics," p. 40) derives the word "Baudekin," "Baldakinus," from Baldak or Bagdad, which "held for no short length of time the lead all over Asia in weaving fine silks, and, in special, golden stuffs."'—'St. Paul's Cathedral,' by W. Sparrow Simpson, D.D. London : E. Stock, 1894. ' Baudekin : tissue or cloth of gold, with figures embroidered in silk (old statute).'—Bailey's Dictionary. Littré, s.v. ' baldaquin,' gives the same etymology.

according as I have read thereof in the chronicles[1] and histories of the kings of Armenia, and have heard from a right truthful knight who was there at the time. In the year of our Lord 1268, when the Tartars had conquered all the kingdoms of the East, Ayco, the then King of Armeniᴀ, of his own accord proceeded to the great Khan, the Emperor of the Tartars, to visit him. Ayco was kindly received by him, because so great and singular an honour had been shown him, that kings should of their own accord visit him and come to meet him, whereat he was much pleased, and honoured the king with many presents. In process of time, when the King of Armenia was about to return home, he asked the Emperor to grant him five boons. First, that the Emperor and all his people should become Christians ; second, that there might always be peace between the Tartars and Armenians ; third, that he would destroy all the churches of Mahomet and consecrate them in honour of God ; fourth, that he would aid him to recover the Holy Land and restore it to the Christians ; and fifth, that he would besiege Baldach and destroy and bring to nought the Caliph, the successor of Mahomet, and his name. To all these demands the Emperor willingly agreed and consented, and fulfilled them in every respect, save only the fourth demand, which was hindered by his death. With regard to the fifth demand, that he should destroy Baldach and the Caliph, he charged his brother Haloon,[2] who then had conquered Persia, that as soon as he had settled the kingdom of Persia, and pro-

---

[1] He probably alludes to ' Haithoni Armeni Historia Orientalis ' in vol. ii. of Vincent of Beauvais's ' Fragmenta.'

[2] Marco Polo calls him ' Houlagou Khan.' He tells the story of how Houlagou offered the Caliph gold to eat, and probably it was from his book that Ludolph copied it. Marino Sanuto improves the story by saying that ' Halao ' poured liquid gold down the Caliph's throat to reproach him for his avarice.

vided for its safe-keeping, he should join the King of
Armenia in besieging Baldach. This he willingly did, and
had no sooner settled the affairs of Persia than he removed
himself to the great city of Nineveh, rested during the
winter, and when the month of March came, went with the
King of Armenia to Baldach and besieged the Caliph.
He charged his four chief captains, each of whom had
thirty thousand Tartars under him, to besiege Baldach
without ceasing until they should take the city, which was
done ; for they took the city on the thirtieth day, slew all
the inhabitants, both young men and old alike, and won
such rich spoils of gold, silver, precious stones, and other
kinds of wealth, as no one ever was heard to have taken in
any city whatsoever. Indeed, out of these spoils the whole
of Tartary has been made rich even to this day, and there
is not now in Tartary a single gold or silver cup that has
not been brought thither from Baldach. Now, when all
were slain or captured, they took the Caliph alive, and
offered him to Haloon, with all his treasure, which was so
great that Haloon feared to look upon it, and in wonder
said to the Caliph, ' How comes it, wretched man, that
thou hast so great a treasure, which I fear even to look
upon ? With it thou mightest have overcome the whole
world, and oughtest to have brought it under thy yoke.
Wherefore didst thou not hire enough troops to defend thy
city ?' The Caliph answered, ' Evil counsel brought this
ruin upon me ; for they said that even women could easily
defend the city against the Tartars.' Then said Haloon,
' Behold, thou art Mahomet's successor, and the teacher
of his law ; I dare not do thee any hurt, neither is it fitting
that thou shouldest live or eat like other men, for out of
thy mouth proceeds the law and doctrine of Mahomet.'
He ordered him to be placed in a fair palace, and poured
out before him gold and silver, precious stones, and pearls,

saying to him, ' Mouth, from whence proceeds so great a law and doctrine, it befits thee to eat such precious food as this.' So the Caliph was shut up in the palace, and on the twelfth day was found dead of hunger ; and after him no Caliph, successor to Mahomet, has arisen in Baldach, even to this day. At present the Emperor of the Tartars rules in Baldach, but its inhabitants are chiefly Saracens dwelling under an exceeding heavy tribute. In these parts I have heard and read many falsehoods about Baldach ; for in these parts men have said, in short, and have had it in writing, that the King of Baldach sent letters to the lords of those parts, and invited them to jousts and tournaments, which is utterly false. There is no man that can remember jousts or tournaments ever to have been held in Baldach, for the people occupy themselves with other things. Near Baldach, at a distance of four days' journey, is another city, which once was called Susa, wherein Ahasuerus flourished. This city, which once was called Susa, is now called Thaurus. In this city there is a dry tree, whereof it is said that the Emperor of the Romans is fated to hang his shield thereon.[1] The people of this city say that no Jew can live or sojourn therein. Not far from Thaurus is another city, named Cambeleth, which also belongs to the Emperor of the Tartars, and it is said that that city is richer and better than all the realm of the Soldan.

XXXIII.—OF THE RIVER NILE.

But to return to my subject : the Nile, one of the rivers of Paradise, flows through Egypt near New Babylon and Damietta, and falls into the Mediterranean Sea near Alexandria. It is bigger and wider than the Rhine, and is very

---

[1] Dicitur quod Imperator Romanorum in ea clipeum suum pendere debeat.

muddy, because it sometimes runs into the ground or into mountains, and is not seen again for two or three miles, and then comes out of the earth again and enters it again, until it comes to Egypt, where it flows straight on. It contains excellent and very fat fishes, and its water is exceeding wholesome ; when first drawn out, it is warm, but when it is put in a jar in the sun it becomes cool, and greatly helps digestion. The sources of this river have never been discovered, beyond what the Holy Scripture[1] says thereof, albeit attempts have often been made. In my time the Soldan kept swimmers who were able to support themselves in the water as naturally as fish. The Soldan promised these men great rewards if they would discover the source of the river, and would bring him a green bough of aloes-wood for a sign. These swimmers went away once upon a time, and did not return for three or four years. Some of them died on the way, and those who returned said that at last the river came down from the mountains with such great force that they could do nothing at all against it. In this river there is an evil beast called a crocodile, which is exceeding strong, fierce, and swift, and does much hurt to those who dwell near him, and to their beasts, and for fear of him it is dangerous to sail upon the Nile. This beast is very great. I have seen a crocodile's skin through which an ox might easily pass. I have been told by a certain Knight Templar that once upon a time the Templars caught a young crocodile and drew his teeth, and that a stone which ten men could not move was tied to his tail, and he drew it alone up to a building that was being made. Yet he is slain by a little worm, which naturally hates him, and follows him whithersoever he goes. The crocodile swallows him, together

---

[1] Under the name of Gihon, Gen. ii. 13.

with other food, and then the worm pierces the crocodile's
heart and slays him. There are likewise many other evil
beasts in the Nile.

XXXIV.—OF THE LAND OF EGYPT.

Now, the land of Egypt is very rich, pleasant, and delightful, abounding beyond all other lands in the world in
trees, fruits, herbs, meadows, and pastures. It is fifteen
days' journey long, and three days' journey wide, and is, I
have been told, like an island, surrounded by the desert
upon three of its sides, and bounded by the Grecian Sea upon
the fourth side. This desert is seven or eight days' journey
wide in its narrowest part. Egypt is an exceeding hot
country, so that winter there can scarce be distinguished
from summer, and roses and other flowers never, or scarce
ever, cease blooming, albeit it never rains there. Its people
have two brazen columns with marks thereon. One of these
they have set up in the middle of the Nile near Babylon,
and the other in the Nile near Alexandria, and when the
river rises so high as to touch the marks on the columns,
then there cannot be any scarcity for two years to come.
Thereupon the Egyptians lead the waters of the Nile
through ditches and channels and passages, and cause
them to run about their land, their fields, woods, gardens,
and orchards, which are then refreshed and watered
throughout, and when the land has been thus watered at
night, the corn and grass will have grown more than a
hand's breadth by morning. At that time the Egyptians
keep watch all that night beside the waters, until all the
land is watered. Every year this river begins to rise thus
in the month of August, and waxes every day until the
Feast of St. Michael, and makes the most desert land
abound with delights and fertility. While the Nile is
rising thus, the people catch all kinds of trees, herbs, and

little birds therein, with nets, more especially aloes-wood and the little birds called parroquets. But where this wood comes from no man has ever found out. It seems that these are old trees, dried up by age, which fall into the water from the mountains. At that time they also take in the Nile shittim wood, which cuts up well like other woods, but cannot be burned. The little green parroquet birds[1] are caught together with the boughs and trees whereon they live, as aforesaid. Some say that they are born in the mountains of Gilboa, which is false ; and they say, too, that they cannot endure water, which also is false, for they are bred upon islands and on the water, and I have seen them swimming on the sea ; but they cannot well endure cold, neither can they keep on flying or swimming for long. This river Nile also has very rich islands in it, abounding in crops and other good things. In Egypt also there are countless fowls, as you have heard already, which are hatched in ovens and in the sun's rays. Likewise in Egypt there are numberless partridges, more than all the birds[2] in this country, and this seems very strange, though there it is common. For sometimes a countryman brings ten thousand partridges with him to market, all of them flying, and when the countryman sits down on the ground they all stop with him, and when he rises and claps his hands they all fly along with him again. If he loses any of them some way off, he whistles with a pipe, and they straightway come back ; and when he comes to the poultry market in the city, he sells as many of them as he can, and takes those which he cannot sell home again with him. A wonderful number of pigeons also are to be seen

---

[1] Haitho, the Armenian, in his 'Historia Orientalis,' chap. v., 'De Regno Indiae,' mentions 'aves qui vocantur papagai.'

[2] Isa. xviii. 1 calls Egypt 'a land shadowing with wings'; but this is usually interpreted to be an allusion to the sails of vessels on the Nile.

in Egypt, and I do not believe that in any place in the world there are so many pigeons as in Egypt. It is altogether forbidden to catch them, for the Soldan and other princes send all their messages by carrier pigeons, wherefore in a short time they know the news and secrets of distant lands. In Egypt also there are numberless deer, so that the fawns of deer and of goats may be found on the roads and in gardens like domestic sheep, and are caught and sold by they who pass by. In Egypt also, even at this day, many cloisters and monasteries, churches and hermitages, are standing entire, but deserted, and excellently well painted, but their paintings have been in many ways spoiled by the Saracens. Likewise in the Egyptian deserts there stand at this day so many cells and hermitages of holy fathers, that in some places, I believe, for two or three (German) miles there is one at every bow-shot. At the present day very many of them are inhabited by Indians, Nubians, and Syrians, living under the rule of St. Antony and St. Macarius. In these deserts God hath wrought great miracles by the hands of the holy fathers, and especially at the place called Stichi,[1] by the hands of St. Antony and St. Macarius, as is told in the 'Lives of the Fathers.' In this desert there is a place beneath an exceeding tall and narrow rock, wherein St. Antony used to dwell, and from out of that rock there flows a stream for half a stone's-throw, until it is lost in the sand, even as running water flows into snow and is seen no more. This place is visited by many for devotion and pleasure, and also by the grace of God and in honour of St. Antony many sicknesses are healed and driven away by this fountain. It is believed to have flowed forth from the rock at his especial prayer, which is clearly true, for it appears to flow no

---

[1] *Solitudinem Scete sive Scithi.* Life of St. Macarius in 'Acta Sanctorum.'

further than was enough to give water to his little cell and little garden. It would take long to tell of the other glories of Egypt, its fertility and its beauty ; but I may add that all sheep, goats, and the like beasts bear young ones twice in the year, and for the most part bear twins at each birth. In Egypt there are three exceeding great cities, which stand beside the Nile, the river of Paradise ; that is to say, New Babylon, Alexandria, and Damietta. This city was of old called Rages,[1] afterwards Edissa, and now Damietta. It was to this city that Tobit[2] of yore sent his son to Gabael. In this city also the body of St. Thomas once lay, and through him God wrought many miracles in the same. In this city[3] also was the letter which Jesus sent to Abgarus, King of this city, wherefore no heretic or infidel was suffered to remain long therein. But afterwards for the sins of the people the city was profaned, and thus at this day it has all been brought to nought. At this day the city has been removed further inland away from the Nile. It was often taken away from the Saracens by St. Louis, the King of the French, and other Christians. But St. Louis was taken prisoner there, and for his ransom the city was given back to the Saracens. Now, since the Saracens had heard that none but Christians could live in the city, they removed the city to another place out of hatred for them. At this day the city is chiefly inhabited by fishermen, and very many merchants come together

[1] ' Regnum Mesopotamiae dilatatur usque ad flumen Euphratem et civitatem Rohais, quae fuit civitas regni Abagari, ad quem fuit transmissa Veronica, quae hodie Romae invenitur.'—Haython, chap. xii.

[2] Tobit v. 7. The city to which Tobit sent his son was Rhey, near Teheran, in Persia.

[3] He has just told us that Damietta was otherwise called Edissa ; he now confuses it with Edessa (Orfa) in Upper Mesopotamia. Marino Sanuto knew where Edessa was, but identified it with Rages (book iii., part vii., chap. i.).

there with their ships, and buy great quantities of fish exceeding cheap, which they export to all parts of the world. Many other wonders may be read of about this city.

XXXV.—OF THE DESERT AND OF MOUNT SINAI.

But to return to my subject : going on from Cairo and Babylon one reaches Sinai in twelve days, for six of which one passes along the road whereof I have just told you, which is full of people, and where there are many things to be seen ; and for six days one passes over the desert, and must carry all things needful upon camels and beasts of burden—to wit, bread, wine, water, meat, biscuits, grapes and raisins, figs, and the like, and, above all, mats to sleep on at night. You must know that the camels, who pass that way every day, know exactly the length of a day's journey and the proper resting-places, and when they come to those places in the evening they lie down on the ground to chew the cud, and will go no further, which is as much as to say to you that this is the proper day's journey and halting-place ; and then they are fed with bread and thorns. A camel is easily fed, and scarce drinks once in three days, whereas if they had to be foraged in proportion to their size, no man could cross the desert with them. After you have crossed the desert you come to the Red Sea, and you must know that the desert is nought but salt and sandy ground, burnt exceeding dry by the sun's heat, and it is rare to find any green thing therein. Howbeit, the desert is not barren in all parts alike, and it is a wondrous thing that whereas its rocks and mountains are very salt, yet the fountains which gush forth therein are very sweet, and are most excellent to drink. Beside these fountains are grass and herbs and the like green things. Near them also one finds the tracks of

lions, dragons, and other dangerous beasts, and especially
of hares. When one has crossed this desert in six days
and beheld its wonders, one comes to the Red Sea, as
aforesaid, when coming from Babylon. The Red Sea has
excellent fishes in large quantities. Its water is not red,
but the earth and bottom thereof is red ; the water appears
red to one looking down upon it because of the red bottom,
but at a distance it is of the same colour as other water,
and its water is exceeding clear and pellucid, so that a
penny can be clearly seen on its bottom at a distance of
twenty stadia, and then because of its red bottom and the
clearness of its water it looks like the clearest red wine.
One finds much coral, many precious stones, and other
things, cast up on its shores. The Red Sea lies in Arabia,
and all the land of Arabia is red, wherefore because of this
redness what things soever grow or are born therein,
save only men, are red. For this cause the purest gold
is found there, like slender roots. Moreover, in the Red
Sea there are many islands, wherein grow red woods of
divers kinds, chief among which is found what is called
here Brazil[1] wood. The Red Sea is not very big, neither
long nor wide, and at the place where the children of Israel
passed over it is scarcely four or five miles wide. In the
Red Sea there is a castle belonging to the Soldan, wherein
noble Christian captives are imprisoned. Moreover, this
castle keeps guard lest any Latin or man from this side of
the sea or born in these parts should pass by it to India,
lest they should bring home any tidings of the power and
condition of the people in parts beyond the sea, or of
Prester John and the Indians, or carry letters to them ;
for it would be easy to sail down the Red Sea to the
ocean and to India if this castle did not stand in the
way. But the Indians and Eastern merchants may pass

[1] Fabri, ii. 656.

that way as often as they please. Howbeit I know bishops and lords who are ever wont to send accounts of this part of the East, and all kinds of news, across the Red Sea to Prester John. The men of this castle are wont to make great nets of leathern thongs, and cast them into the sea. Then they let the coral, which grows in the sea like a plant, entangle itself among the thongs, and every half-year they pull it up full of countless and most splendid corals, whereby they make vast gain all for nothing. Through this Red Sea comes much precious merchandise from India, and this is taken through that branch of the sea which runs out of the Red Sea, and down the Nile to all parts of the world. As I have said already, by going thus round about the shore of the Red Sea one comes to the place where the children of Israel crossed over the sea when pursued by the Egyptians, and on this journey one finds many rare things of divers sorts on the beach. Thus, after leaving many mountains behind, and seeing many wondrous sights, one comes to the well of Marah,[1] where the water was salt when the children of Israel passed that way, and by casting in wood was at God's bidding made sweet. Going on from Marah through various places, after seeing and leaving behind many mountains, one comes to Elim,[2] where when the children of Israel passed that way there were seventy palm-trees and twelve wells. This place is very fertile and very beautiful; one can also see that many cells of holy fathers and hermitages once stood near it. Leaving Elim, one comes into the wilderness of Sin, to Mount Sinai. An exceeding great and fair convent has been built at the foot of this mountain, in the place where Moses saw the burning bush which was not consumed, and God spoke to him out of the bush; it is roofed with lead, fenced with iron doors, and well fortified in every

---

[1] Exod. xv. 23.   [2] Exod. xv. 27.

way. In it are more than four hundred Greek, Georgian,
and Arab monks, both clerical and lay, who do not always
abide in the monastery, but are scattered abroad here and
there, working at the business affairs of the monastery.
By great toil they get what is needful both for themselves
and for pilgrims, and right faithfully distribute the same to
pilgrims ; they live most devout, strict, and chaste lives, in
humble obedience to their Archbishop and prelates, dwelling
in all holiness and righteousness in all things. They rarely
drink wine save on especial feast-days, never eat flesh, but
feed on salads, vegetables, beans, dates, and the like, with
water, vinegar, and salt, in one refectory without table-
furniture. They most devoutly celebrate Divine service
daily and nightly according to their rite, and in all things
follow the rule of St. Antony. The lay brethren work
very hard, burning charcoal on the mountains, and bring-
ing dates from Elim in great quantities on the backs of
camels and beasts of burden to Babylon, where they sell
them, and there ample alms and presents are made to them
by the Christians and merchants dwelling there. Without
this so many people could not support themselves in a
desert place, nor could they afford the costly hospitality
which they so liberally and kindly bestow upon pilgrims ;
but they fetch dates from Elim and charcoal from the
mountains, a distance of more than twelve days' journey,
and sell them, as I have told you already. In this monastery stands an exceeding fair church, which they keep very
clean within, and light with many lamps and lights of
divers kinds, and hold in especial reverence the place
where the high altar stands. They put off their shoes
before entering this place, and make pilgrims who wish to
enter it put off their shoes likewise ; for in the place where
the high altar now is once stood the burning bush, out of
which God said unto Moses, ' Put off thy shoes from thy

feet, for the place whereon thou standest is holy ground.'[1] In this church, on the right-hand side of the high altar, but in a higher place, stands a kind of chest of white marble, wherein are placed and enclosed the head and the bones of the glorious virgin Catharine, mixed together in disorder, which bones were translated thither from the top of Mount Sinai. This head and bones are displayed very solemnly by the Archbishop and other prelates of the monastery, with censers, candles, and acolytes; and at these times the Saracen guides and camel-drivers and grooms who come with the pilgrims earnestly beg that they, too, may be allowed to see these holy and wondrous bones, and kneel with the greatest devotion by the side of the Christians. When the bones are thus being shown to the pilgrims, if there be a bishop or other prelate among the pilgrims, then the Archbishop or chief prelate of the monastery takes one of the holy bones in his hand, and rubs it hard with a silver instrument shaped like a rod, whereupon oil[2] bursts forth from the pores like sweat. In the chest wherein the holy bones are enclosed, there has been formed in one corner a cavity into which all the oil that runs out of all the bones flows and gathers. There is always a silver spoon in this cavity, which the prelate who shows the bones takes in his hand, fills little glass phials with the oil, and gives each pilgrim a little phial with oil therein. Moreover, in this monastery there are very many other venerable relics, yet the monks of the monastery could not exist there save by the especial grace of God, for divers reasons caused by the instigation of the devil. For this cause there never is any jealousy or discord among them, but they are in favour with all who see them, as well with Saracens as with Christians, and especially with the Soldan, who is wont to bestow great alms upon them.

[1] Exod. iii. 5.   [2] Anon., i. 3.

So in their labours and continual passage over the desert they never are hurt by any dangers or by fierce beasts, neither are they troubled or made sick either in summer or winter by unseasonable weather or excessive heat of the sun. They have even, I believe, obtained an especial grace, whereby certain unclean creatures, such as flies, wasps, hornets, fleas, and the like, cannot live there, or enter the walls of the convent.[1] A monk of that convent of rare learning told me that once upon a time, at the instigation of the devil and by Divine permission, these creatures did them as much harm as they could, and they suffered so many and such grievous torments and molestations from unclean creatures of this sort, that they even thought of leaving the place, but by the holy counsel of one of the monks they took courage, and prayed to God that of His mercy He would drive away and remove all such creatures from them. This prayer was straightway granted by Him, and from that time forth they have never noticed any such creatures whatsoever within the walls of the monastery, albeit without the walls they do most grievous hurt both to men and beasts. Moreover, it has often been proved that such unclean creatures when carried alive within the walls die straightway. All these privileges the brethren have obtained by their holy and righteous lives, for they do not serve the pilgrims for money or out of greed, but to all who come thither and for as long as they please to stay there, whether they be rich or poor, high or low, the brethren give all that they themselves have, simply and kindly, in God's name ; and should anyone offer to give them, or any one of them, any present, they altogether refuse and reject it, and should any one of them take it, he would be severely punished. So also when the pilgrims are leaving them they most kindly, and

---

[1] Sir John Maundeville, chap. v. ; Fabri, ii. 551.

without any charge, give each one of them loaves of bread,
beans, and the like, according to the best of their ability,
for each day of his journey, until he shall reach the
dwellings of men, and this they do alike to rich and poor,
high and low. These monks hold the Feast of St. Gregory
the Pope in especial reverence above all other feasts, for
during the time when he was head of the Church he
supported them by gifts from the treasury of the Church,
and encouraged them to dwell there, and from that time
forth they have remained four hundred in number, though
before they were few.

Above this monastery towers Mount Sinai, up which one
climbs by many steps with greater toil than words can
express. At the top of this mount a church stands on the
spot where God said to Elijah the prophet, 'What dost
thou here, Elijah?' as we read in the Book of Kings.
Near this there is another chapel in the place where the
law was given to Moses, and the glory of the Lord appeared
to him. At this place there is still to be seen a cavity in
the hard rock, wherein the image of Moses is engraved as
in a seal. It was in this cavity that God stretched forth
His right hand over Moses when He passed by in His
majesty and showed Moses His hinder parts, because
Moses could not abide the splendour of His face. It was
to the top of another taller mountain beside a deep valley
in the same place that the body of the glorious virgin
Catharine was borne by angels from Alexandria, and
miraculously discovered by the hermits who dwelt thereon.
This same mount is most toilsomely climbed and visited,
but on its top there is no chapel, or oratory, or dwelling,
I suppose because the ascent is so difficult that human
hands could not build anything there. But there may be
seen the place where St. Catharine's body was found,
where there is the mark of human shoulders on the rock,

and this place is marked with stones. Upon this mount God wrought many wonders, all of which it would take long to tell. You must know that Mount Sinai exceeds all the other mountains of those parts in height, and, as I have said, one climbs it with exceeding great toil, more than any tongue can tell, up very many[1] exceeding narrow steps cut out of the rock. On the side towards Egypt it loses the name of Sinai, and is called Horeb. From its top all the countries round about can be easily viewed, and at that height a man is greatly affected by the air ; from thence one can narrowly examine the Red Sea, Elim, the place where it rained manna upon the children of Israel, and all the other places in the neighbourhood. At the foot of the mount is a fair plain, whereon Moses used to feed the flock of his father-in-law Jethro, and there he saw the burning bush. It was on this plain also that Israel fought against Amalek,[2] while Moses prayed with uplifted hands, and Joshua (Aaron) and Ur stayed up his hands. It was likewise on this plain that the children of Israel made themselves a molten calf, whereof the Bible tells us. On this plain also the fire consumed Nadab and Abihu,[3] and many places may be seen round about it of which the Scriptures make mention.

XXXVI.—OF THE WILDERNESS OF SINAI.

From Mount Sinai one journeys on toward Syria across the wilderness in thirteen days, taking some provisions of one's own, and being given some by the convent. This wilderness is very bad and dangerous. It lies in Arabia, and all this land, whether it be habitable or desert, is called

---

[1] The 'Commemoratorium de Casis Dei' says that there were 7,700 steps. See Tobler's excellent note in his 'Descriptiones Terrae Sanctae,' p. 384.

[2] Exod. xvii.   [3] Lev. x. 1.

Arabia.   In this wilderness there is exceeding great scarcity
of water, and countless people dwell therein like wild beasts.
They are called Bedouins, and move about in companies
of hundreds and of thousands together, dwelling in tents
made of felt or leather,[1] and roaming to and fro about the
wilderness with their cattle and beasts of burden, pasturing
them in whatever places they can find water, though it
be only a little, in wells and runnels, and living on the
milk of their camels and flocks.   They never eat bread,
unless some pilgrims chance to give them some, or unless
it be brought to them more than twelve days' journey ; for
they neither sow nor reap, but live like wild beasts, and
their faces are dreadful to look upon, black, and bearded ;
they are very fierce and swift, and on the backs of their
dromedaries they can go as far as they please in one day,
seeking for the places where water may be found.   They
wind an exceeding long linen cloth round their heads
because of the unbearable heat of the sun, and they use
bows and arrows.   In this wilderness water can scarce be
found for two or three days' journey together, and in
places where it is found on one day it will be dried up on
another.   Moreover, in this wilderness, in places which are
altogether flat for one hour, in another hour a monstrous
hill of sand[2] may be heaped up and gathered together, first
in one place and then in another, never continuing in one
stay, wherefore the road across the wilderness can never
be known save by the mountains, and from the Bedouins,
who know and understand the roads in the wilderness even
as men know the way about their own houses.   These[3]

---

[1] ' Sub tentoriis de filtris et pellibus.'   Wilhelm von Boldinsel, as
well as Ludolph, has these words.

[2] Fabri, ii. 469.

[3] 'Parum curant de Soldano ; ipse tamen caute capitaneos eorum
trahit ad se muneribus et hujusmodi, quia, ut dicitur, quando cultores
hujus deserti vellent et essent unanimes, possent Ægyptum et Syriam
de facili occupare.'—W. von Boldinsel.

Bedouins care nothing for the Soldan, and render him no
obedience whatever ; but the Soldan cautiously tempts
and quiets them with presents, even when they dwell far
away from him ; for if they chose they could with the
greatest ease conquer and ruin the whole of the Soldan's
kingdom. The Virgin Mary crossed this wilderness with
the Child Jesus, when she fled from Judaea from before the
face of Herod, and all along the road whereby she is
believed to have passed there grow dry roses which in these
parts are called roses of Jericho. The Bedouins gather
these roses in the wilderness and sell them to pilgrims for
bread ; moreover, the Saracen women are very glad to have
these roses by them, and when about to be delivered they
drink the water which has been poured over the roses, and
declare that they are most useful and valuable during
pregnancy.[1] In this wilderness there are many other
perils, whereof it would take long to tell, from winds,
sands, savage men, serpents, lions, dragons, and other
venomous and dangerous beasts. Now, after crossing this
wilderness, which lies to the southward, one comes to the
beginning of the Promised Land, to a city, once fair but
now deserted, called Beersheba. It appears that this city
was once adorned with many fair churches, whereof some
remain standing at this day.

XXXVII.—HEBRON, THE VALE OF MAMBRE, AND BETHLEHEM.

Going on from Beersheba at mid-day, one comes to a
fair and ancient city, still tolerably populous, named
Hebron. On the side of a hill near this city there stands
a fair church, wherein is the double cave[2] wherein the
three patriarchs, Abraham, Isaac, and Jacob, are buried

---

[1] John of Hildesheim, chap. xxiii.   [2] Gen. xxiii. 17.

together with their wives. This church is held especially sacred by the Saracens, and they will not suffer any Christian to enter it, but let them pray at the door. They suffer Jews to enter, which in my time they paid money to do. Howbeit this church can be viewed by Christians both inside and out, and within it is whitewashed and well adorned with stones, and one goes downstairs as into a cellar, into the cave where the patriarchs and their wives are buried. Near Hebron is the field of whose earth Adam was made, and the more of that earth is dug up and carried away, the more it fills up of its own accord. This earth is carried away to distant lands, and some say that it is sold, but about that I know nothing for certain. Near Hebron also is the vale of Mambre, where Abraham sat at the door of his tent and saw three[1] and worshipped one. In my time there were in Hebron three renegades, from the diocese of Minden, it was said. Two of them were esquires,[2] and the third was their servant. One of them carried water on his shoulders and sold it in the street, as is the custom in those parts; another laboured with his hands and got his living as best he could; the third, who was their servant, was a soldier, because he was thought a better-looking fellow in every way by the Soldan's officers. When asked why they had renounced their faith, they replied that they had hoped that their lord would obtain riches and honour, but he had disappointed them, and they declared with groans that they would willingly steal away out of the country if they could; for they were leading a most wretched life. They had not the heart to tell who they

---

[1] Gen. xviii. 1, 2. Compare W. von Boldinsel, chap. v. ; and Anon., vi., p. 38, note.

[2] *Domicelli.* I find in 'Littré's Dictionary,' '*Damoiseau :* titre donné autrefois à un jeune gentilhomme qui n'était pas encore reçu chevalier. . . . Etym. anc. Liegois, *damesheal ;* Prov. *donzel,* etc., etc., du bas Latin *dominicellus,* diminutif de *dominus,* seigneur.'

had formerly been. These three men were very friendly with a certain knight in those parts, named William de Bolensele (*sic*), who lay in over - sea parts before my time, and was greatly honoured there by the Soldan and other kings and princes. I have heard that he died at Cologne.[1] Going on from Hebron, one easily reaches Bethlehem in one day. On this day's road once stood the monastery of St. Karioth the Abbot.[2] When the time of his dissolution was at hand, his monks, seeing him to be in the last agony, said, ' After the death of our Abbot St. Karioth, shall we live any longer upon earth ?' And at that very word they all ,entered upon their last agony and died, and remained for a long time uncorrupt, standing as though in the death-agony, neither were the Saracens able to destroy them, albeit they often tried ; but now the convent is desolate, and no traces of them remain. Bethlehem is an exceeding fair and pleasant village, not a long one, standing upon a mountain ridge, and almost entirely inhabited by Christians. It abounds with pastures, grass, and herbs, and is well fenced by valleys all round about ; wherefore the King of Jerusalem and the Christians were always wont to gather together their armies there. Its people have abundance of wine and other good things. In Bethlehem[3] stands a great and very fair church, most

[1] Wilhelm von Boldinsel landed at Tyre in 1332, was at Jerusalem on May 5, 1333, and wrote his book in the spring of 1336. A letter of his, dated Avignon, Michaelmas Day, 1337, is extant, in which he states his intention of coming to Cologne.

[2] Anon., p. 62, note ; p. 72.

[3] ' Super tugurium et speluncam nativitatis domini Helena pulcherrimam fundavit ecclesiam opere mosayco, marmoribus auro et vitro regaliter et ditissime ornatam, in modum castri cum propugnaculis factam ; sed non est testudinata, sed super ligna et tigna cedrina est plumbo cooperta. et in hac ecclesia ante chorum descenditur ad speluncam in qua Christus natus est, et non longe ab altari quod ibidem est, est presepium trium vel quatuor pedum, in quo Christus infantulus fuit reclinatus ; et in ipsa spelunca S. Ieronymus

excellently fortified with many towers and outworks like a castle. It is roofed with lead ; it is adorned with mosaic work of jasper, marble, and gold, beyond, I believe, any other church under the sun, and is in every way built most richly, nobly, and royally, as it is meet that it should be. It possesses about seventy precious marble columns, and is not vaulted, but roofed beneath the lead with most noble wood, and beams and planks of cedar. The walls of the church are gilded under glass, and wondrously wrought with painted glass. Before my time the Saracens wanted to carry off some of the columns, but were much frightened by a vision,[1] and let them stand, nor did they ever try to take them away afterwards. In front of the choir in this church one goes down some steps into a stone cave, not built, but natural, wherein, immediately beneath the high altar, is the place where for our sake God was made man of a virgin mother. On the place itself there stands an altar, and not far from the altar stands the manger wherein the Blessed Virgin Mary laid the Infant Jesus, wrapped in swaddling clothes, very God and man weeping in human weakness even as children are wont to weep. Near the manger may still be seen irons fixed in the marble with lead, wherein were iron rings to which the country people tied their beasts of burden and cattle when they came to market. The manger is of stone, about four palms long, as is the custom in that land. St. Jerome is buried in this cave. On the night of the Nativity all nations under

Paula et Eustochium sunt sepulti.   et in ista ecclesia sunt lxx columpne marmoree ; et anno dñi M°ccc°xli° Sarraceni pulchriores columpnas excipere voluerunt et in templo suo ponere, sed horribili visione perterriti ipsas stare permiserunt.' — John of Hildesheim's ' Historia iii Regum,' chap. xxxviii.

[1] See John of Hildesheim, in preceding note ; Fabri, i. 598. The date in the preceding note, 1341, must be wrong, as Marino Sanuto, who wrote before that date, tells the same story. The legend was probably a much older one, possibly connected with serpent worship.

heaven assemble there, as is very right, and each nation has a particular place in this church set apart for itself for ever wherein to celebrate Divine service according to its own rite. The Latins have now the place wherein God was made man, and in like manner each separate nation has its own separate place. In my time the Nubians had not as yet any place of their own, but the Soldan had a chapel especially built for them. Before this church stands the monastery in which St. Jerome, St. Paula, and Eustochium, and very many other saints once dwelt, and by the grace of God wrought many miracles. A Saracen now dwells on this spot, and receives one Venetian penny from anyone who wants to go into the church. Also at Bethlehem there is an underground chapel beneath the rock, which seems to have had two doors, and therefore one could pass straight through it, but now one door has been built up. In this pit, which now is a chapel, the Blessed Virgin lay hid for three days for fear of Herod, and suckled the Child Jesus there. In her fear she chanced to let fall some of her milk[1] upon a stone in that place,

---

[1] See Fabri, i. 563, in this series, and Marino Sanuto, iii., xiv. 11 ; also Abbot Daniel, p. 41. In John of Hildesheim's ' Historia Trium Regum,' chap. xxvii., I find the following : ' Post recessum trium regum beata virgo cum infantulo Jhesu in tugurio aliquantulum permansit, sed crescente de ipsa et de tribus Regibus tam mirabili fama, tunc de ipso tugurio in aliam spelunca subterraneam cum infantulo Jhesu metu Judeorum intravit, et usque ad diem purificacionis sue permansit in ea : et quia omnes eam diligebant, prout poterant ipsam colebant et necessaria ei ministrabant ; in qua spelunca post modum facta est capella in honore iii Regum at S. Nycholai consecrata. et videtur per ipsam capellam communis transitus fuisse, et ii januas habuisse, sed una jam lapidibus est obstructa. et in illa capella videtur adhuc lapis super quem beata virgo sedendo Filium lactare consuevit. et quadam vice modicum lactis de sua mamilla super lapidem cecidit, cujus lactis species usque in presentem illem super ipsum lapidem permansit, et quanto plus abraditur tanto plus crescit.'—John of Hildesheim, edited by C. Horstmann, in the Early English Text Society. See also ' Guide-book,' p. 26, note.

which milk is there even to this day. The milk oozes out of the stone like moisture, and is a milky colour with a tinge of red. The more of the milk is scraped off, the more is restored in the same quantity, and no more. This is the milk which may be seen, and is shown in many different churches; for. it is taken away hither and thither by the pilgrims. Also near Bethlehem there is a great cave in the rock, into which a great number of bodies of the Innocents were cast, and this rock has been almost entirely carried away by pilgrims. Moreover, one mile from Bethlehem is the place where St. Jerome was especially wont to dwell, and where he translated many books from Hebrew, Chaldee, and Greek into Latin. Near Bethlehem also, half a mile away toward Sodom and Gomorrah, is the place where the angels announced to the shepherds that God was born as man. In this place there has been built an exceeding fair double church, which is called *Gloria in excelsis,* which the angels sang there. For this cause in Bethlehem also they begin all the canonical hours of the day with *Gloria in excelsis,* just as we do with *Deus in adjutorium.*[1] And they begin all Masses, even Masses for the souls of the dead, with *Gloria in excelsis deo,* by special custom, as I have often seen in their service-book. This is Bethlehem, the city of God most high, wherein David was born, whereof also the prophet Micah said, 'And thou Bethlehem, in the land of Juda, art not the least among the princes of Juda.'[2] For Bethlehem

[1] 'In loco etiam in quo pastoribus angelus Christum natum annunciavit; ipsa duplicem ecclesiam pulcherriman construxit, quam Gloria in excelsis vocavit; que ecclesia fuit quondam ditissimum collegium canonicorum, qui ex speciali privilegio omnes horas canonicas cum "Gloria in excelsis deo,' etc., inceperunt, sicud nos per "Deus in adjutorium," et adhuc incipiunt ibidem horas cum "Gloria in excelsis."' —John of Hildesheim, chap. xxxvii.

[2] Micah v. 2; Matt. ii. 6.

stands in the midst of Judah, wherefore the whole of that land is called Judaea; but the land which once was called Judaea is now called Syria, and its people are called Syrians. From Bethlehem one goes on to Jerusalem, by a road on the left of which is the tomb of Jacob's wife Rachel, at the place where she bore Benjamin, and died in childbirth. Near this road is the aforesaid church called *Gloria in excelsis,* and also beside this road there are and have been very many cells of saints, churches and caves, monasteries and tombs, belonging to the Christians. Here God has wrought many miracles through these saints, and to this day very many incorrupt bodies of saints, whose names God alone knows,[1] are found in divers places in the caves and grottos. Also near this road is the place where was the pit into which Joseph was cast by his brethren, and sold to the Ishmaelites. After seeing these and many other sights, one arrives at Jerusalem, and the distance between the two places is only three of the short miles of the country.

XXXVIII.—THE HOLY CITY JERUSALEM.

Jerusalem, the holy city, wherein our redemption was wrought, stands on a mount in a wholesome air. It is well fenced on the north side by walls, towers, and outworks, on the east by the Valley of Jehoshaphat, and on the south and west by other deep valleys; but it lacks water within the walls, and its cisterns are filled by water which is brought from Hebron by underground aqueducts and channels, which may clearly be seen by the side of that road as one journeys along it. This glorious city is

[1] Dr. F. J. Bliss tells us that the Armenian inscription on the mosaic pavement found at Jerusalem in June, 1894, is to the effect that the place was in memory of the salvation of all those Armenians whose name the Lord knows (Quarterly Statement, P.E.F., October, 1894).

not over-long or over-wide, neither is it too great or too small, but it is tolerably well built, and has been somewhat removed to the east of where it stood at the time of Christ's crucifixion, by Aelius Hadrianus, after its destruction by Titus and Vespasian, to show honour to the place of Calvary. In Jerusalem stand the Lord's Temple and Solomon's Temple, and they alone take up a great part of the city. The Saracens suffer no Christian to enter this temple, and if they do enter they must either die or renounce their faith. This came to pass in my time, for some Greeks got in and trampled upon the Saracens' books. As they refused to renounce their faith, they were cut in two. The Lord's Temple is round, built in the Greek fashion, very tall and large, roofed with lead, and made of great hewn and polished stones. Upon its pinnacle the Saracens have after their fashion placed a crescent moon. This temple also has a great fore-court, which is not roofed in, but well paved and adorned with white marble. Near this temple, on the right hand, there is an oblong church with a lead roof, which is called Solomon's Porch. The Saracens pay the greatest reverence to the Lord's Temple, keeping it exceeding clean both within and without, and all alike entering it unshod. They call it ' the holy Rock,' not ' the Temple,' and therefore they say to one another, ' Let us go to the holy Rock.' They do not say, ' Let us go to the Temple.' They call the temple ' the holy Rock ' because of a little rock which stands in the midst of the temple, fenced about with an iron railing. I have heard it said of a truth by Saracen renegades that no Saracen presumes to touch that rock, and that Saracens journey from distant lands to devoutly visit it. Indeed, God has deigned to show respect to this rock in divers ways, and has wrought many miracles thereon, as the Bible bears

witness to us both in the Old and New Testament. First
of all, it was upon this rock that Melchisedech, the first
priest, offered bread and wine. Also it was upon this
rock that Jacob slept and saw God's glory, and a ladder
standing upon this rock, whose top reached to heaven, and
the angels of God ascending and descending the same.
Also it was upon this rock that David saw the angel
standing with a bloody sword in his hand, and stayin͛
from the slaughter of the people.[1] It was upon this rock
that the priests used to lay the burnt sacrifices, which often
were consumed by fire from heaven. It was within this
rock that Jeremiah the prophet is believed to have
miraculously enclosed the Ark of the Covenant when the
people were removed to Babylon, saying, 'As for that
place, it shall be unknown until the time that God gather
His people together again, and receive them unto mercy,'[2]
and therein it is believed to have remained even to this
day. Upon this rock Christ was presented when a child,
and was given into the arms of the Just Simeon and
was received by him. It was upon this rock that Christ
disputed with the Jews when He was a boy of twelve years
of age, and His parents lost Him; from this rock He
often taught the people and often preached. The Lord's
Temple, we read, was built by Solomon on the threshing-
floor of Ornan, and albeit it has been destroyed by many,
yet it has always been rebuilt on the same spot, in the
same form, and with the same stones. God, moreover, has
greatly honoured and glorified this Temple, and greatly
loved it. It was from this Temple that Solomon saw

[1] 2 Sam. xxiv. 16 ; 2 Chron. iii. 1.

[2] 2 Macc. ii. 5, 6 ; but we are told in verse 4 that the prophet took
the ark 'to the mountain where Moses climbed up and saw the
heritage of God.' And Fabri, vol. ii., 182, 233, points out the place in
the valley of 'Galmoab' (Vulgate), 'a valley in the land of Moab,
over against Bethpeor,' Deut. xxxiv. 6 (A.V.).

smoke going up and the glory of God abiding over it.   In
this Temple Joseph's rod flowered.   In this Temple the
Blessed Virgin Mary was presented, and made her offering
after her betrothal.   In this temple Christ was presented,
and was set upon its pinnacle,[1] and tempted by the (evil)
spirit.   Out of this Temple also Christ cast those who
bought and sold ; He often taught and disputed therein,
and wrought many miracles, as is testified by the Gospels.
Christ also consecrated this Temple by His glorious
presence, and therein in our weakness He suffered much
abuse and much ill-usage at the hands of the Jews.   It
was from this Temple that St. James the Less, our Lord's
brother, was cast down and martyred.   Near this Temple,
on the left hand thereof, is the ancient Golden Gate,
through which on Palm Sunday Jesus entered riding upon
an ass.   To this gate on every Palm Sunday, even to this
day, a solemn procession of Christians is made before sunrise, and over this gate boys sing *Gloria, laus,* etc.   Then
the Archbishop of the Armenians enters the gate on an
ass, and is welcomed by the boys and the people even as
Christ was there welcomed by the Jews.   A little way to
the north of this Temple there is a church on the spot
where the Blessed Virgin Mary was born, and on that
same spot St. Anne and Joachim her husband lie buried in
an underground cave.   In front of this church stands the
sheep-pool, having five porticos round about it, wherein
the sick used to be healed when the waters were troubled
by an angel, as the Gospel bears witness.   At this day
there is a cave there, wherein when it rains all the water
from the city collects together.   Out of this Church of St.
Mary the Saracens have now made a church of their own.
Yet all the story of Anna and Joachim and the Blessed
Mary's birth remains to this day right nobly painted on

[1] See my note to Anon., p. 66.

the front of the church. This painting in my time used to be all devoutly and religiously explained to Christians by an old Saracen woman named Baguta. She used to dwell over against the church, and declared that the picture of Joachim stood for Mahomet, and the painting of the trees for paradise, wherein Mahomet kissed girls, and she referred the whole of the painting to Mohammed, and set it forth with fervour, and would tell many more and more wondrous stories about Mahomet with tears in her eyes. Not far from the Lord's Temple, on the south side, below the city, is the hill of Sion, which is a little higher than the rest of the ground whereon the city stands. It was on this mount that of old stood the city of David, whereof the Scripture makes mention. Upon this Mount Sion, or in this city of David, there once was built an exceeding fair monastery called the Convent of St. Mary on Mount Sion, wherein were canons regular. Within this monastery were enclosed all the following holy places.[1] First of all in this place Christ supped with His disciples and celebrated the first Easter, made His testament and revealed His betrayer, while the beloved disciple lay upon His breast and drank in the secrets of heaven. Also in this same place Christ humbly washed His disciples' feet and dried them with a napkin, and, though He was their Lord and Master, gave them an example of humility. Christ also frequently visited this place while in the flesh, and it was here that after His death and resurrection He appeared to His disciples as they sat with closed doors, and was seen there once again ; there Thomas the unbelieving thrust his fingers into His side. Here also the Blessed Mary and the disciples were sitting grieving, with the doors closed for fear of the Jews, when they received the Holy Ghost the Comforter. Here also after the

[1] Fabri, i. 289 et seq.

Lord's Passion the Blessed Mary often dwelt; in this
place she rendered up her spirit to her Son, and here all
the disciples were miraculously assembled. In this place
also St. Matthias was wondrously chosen an Apostle.
Here also the beloved disciple often celebrated Mass with
the Blessed Mary, and dwelt here with St. Mary and
St. Luke until the Blessed Mary's death. Here also St.
Stephen was buried between Nicodemus and Abybos. In
this place also David and Solomon and the other kings of
Judah are buried, and their sepulchres may be seen at
this day. In this monastery there now dwell Minorite
brethren, who in my time were amply furnished with
necessaries by Queen Sancea, the wife of King Robert,[1]
and there they publicly and devoutly hold Divine service,
except that they are not allowed to preach publicly to
Saracens, and they bury their dead without the knowledge of the officers of the city. These brethren were in
my time exceeding prosperous men. Foreign merchants,
and even Saracens, praised them much, for they did good
offices to all men.

At the foot of this mount there stands an exceeding
strong castle, called David's Castle, which is believed to
have remained standing from the time of David, for when
the city was destroyed by Titus and Vespasian, the
Mount Sion and this castle stood without the city. This
castle was once held by the Patriarch of Jerusalem, but
now is inhabited by an officer of the Soldan, and is most
carefully guarded by him and his mercenaries. At the
foot of this mount there is also a church called St. Saviour's,
wherein is the stone which the angel rolled away from the

---

[1] This King, according to Dr. F. Deycks, must have been either
Charles Robert of Anjou, King of Hungary, or Robert Bruce, King of
Scotland. I think that, after reading Fabri's account (ii. 379) of the
Minorite convent on Mount Sion, one is inclined to think that Ludolph
meant Rupert, King of Apulia, Calabria, Sicily, and Jerusalem.

sepulchre, which is there publicly shown. Near this mount
also St. James the Great was beheaded, and over the spot
a church has been built, wherein now is the Archbishop of
the Armenians and canons of the Roman obedience. Also
in Jerusalem there is another church called St. Mary the
Latin. In Jerusalem, moreover, there are many churches
of schismatics and heretics, and very many other holy
places and gracious oratories. Above the Mount Calvary
and Christ's sepulchre a great and fair church has been
built, nobly decorated with marble, mosaic work, paintings,
and other ornaments. It has towers in front of the choir
and above the same, and it is open above the place of
Christ's sepulchre. The inside of this church is very much
like the cathedral of Munster in Westphalia, especially in
the choir. In this church, near the choir, on the south side,
is Mount Calvary, where Jesus was crucified. One ascends
this mount at the present day by some stairs within the
church, and once one used also to ascend thither by some
stairs outside the church, but this door has now been
blocked up on the outside. This mount is formed of
exceeding hard rock, and beneath the mount is the chapel
of the Nubians, cut out of the solid rock. On the top of
Mount Calvary also there is a chapel, to which one ascends
from within the church, and in the place where Jesus was
crucified there is the hole in which the cross was placed,
and the rending of the solid rock which came to pass at
the time of Christ's Passion may still be plainly seen.
Also in this same chapel are buried those right glorious
princes, Godfrey, Duke of Bouillon, and Baldwin, his
brother, the first Christian Kings of Jerusalem, who won
the Holy Land with exceeding great toil, and puissantly
recovered and held the same, wrought the Saracens in-
estimable hurt, and bestowed the greatest boons upon
Christendom. It is a great wonder that the Saracens

suffer their sepulchres and bodies to rest undisturbed in such honour, seeing how much harm they did them, and how they even took away from them the whole of the Holy Land; for in Lombardy, when Christians quarrel, they cast one another's rotten corpses to the dogs. These same glorious princes made a rule that no King of Jerusalem should wear a golden crown, but a crown of thorns, which rule their successors observe even to this day. On this Mount Calvary the story of Christ's Passion is read every day, when any Christians are dwelling there, as I have clearly read in their service-book. Near Mount Calvary, where now there is a cupboard, is the place where His mother and the disciples and the other women stood, and there Jesus commended his mother to the care of His disciple, saying, 'Woman, behold thy son.' In front of the door of the choir, on the south side, there is a black stone, which is the place whereon they laid Jesus's body when they took Him down from the cross and wrapped Him in linen cloths. In front of the choir, on the west side, stands a small double chapel which has as it were three doors, and wherein three altars seem to have stood. From this first chapel one goes into another chapel, wherein is Christ's sepulchre, through a low and small doorway, arched semicircularly, and made so that one must enter it with a bent back. This chapel is semicircularly vaulted; it has no window, and in it is Christ's sepulchre. The length of this chapel and sepulchre is about nine palms, the width of the chapel about seven palms, and the height of the chapel about twelve palms. Christ's sepulchre[1] is cut out of the solid rock, but lest it

[1] Wilhelm von Boldinsel observes (chap. vii.) that 'Monumentum Christi excisum erat in petra viva . . . istud vero ex pluribus est compositum et de novo conglutinatum cemento minus artificialiter et minus quam decet ordinate.'

should be defiled or carried away by pilgrims, it is covered with other stones of white marble. The stone which covers it on the front side has three holes pierced through it, and through those holes one can kiss the true sepulchre and the true stone thereof. This stone wherewith the sepulchre is cased is so cunningly joined on to the sepulchre, that to the ignorant it seems to be all one stone. For this reason I do not believe that there is in any church a piece of the true stone of Christ's sepulchre; for with the exception of those places whereof you have heard, it is and ever has been kept most carefully guarded. Indeed, if Christ's sepulchre could be carried away in grains of sand, it would have been so carried away long ago, even had it been a great mountain, so that scarce one grain of sand would have remained on the spot. Now, as for the lamps and candlesticks which are said to be round about the holy sepulchre, I declare that there is no lamp or candlestick whatever round about the sepulchre; but there dwell in the Church of the Holy Sepulchre ancient Georgians who have the key of the chapel of the holy sepulchre, and food, alms, candles, and oil for lamps to burn round about the holy sepulchre are given them by pilgrims through a little window in the south door of the church, and if this should fail it remains without any light whatsoever, and is altogether without honour and respect, for the Saracens have as much respect for Christ's sepulchre as Christians have for a Jewish synagogue. In this church also, in front of the choir, a little way to the southward, there is the place where the three Maries ·stood and said to one another, ' Who shall roll away the stone for us from the mouth of the sepulchre?' Also in this same church stands one part of the pillar to which Jesus was bound and scourged; the other part is at Constantinople.

In this church also one goes down forty steps to the

place where the three crosses were found, and in this
lower part, in the chapel, stands the episcopal chair of
James the Less, wherein he used to sit as Bishop of
Jerusalem. In this church also stand the pillars which at
the time of Christ's Passion stood in Pilate's house, which
pillars from that time to this present have never ceased to
sweat forth water. Furthermore, in this church there is
the place where the dead man was laid upon Christ's cross,
and was raised up to life. In this church also is the place
where Jesus appeared to Mary Magdalen in the likeness
of a gardener. All these holy places are enclosed within
this church, and the church is like a palace prepared for
the various needs of pilgrims and of those who are locked
up therein ; for pilgrims who visit it are locked up therein
from the first hour of one day till the same hour of the
following day, and can inspect everything to their hearts'
content. Twice a year—that is to say, from Good Friday
to Monday after Easter, and from the Eve of the Invention
of the Holy Cross till the morrow of the feast—the
Christians who dwell there are let into the church for
nothing, and locked in, and then one finds shops in the
church where sundry things and victuals are sold, even as
in this country they do in markets and fairs, and then
one hears talk and songs in divers tongues. Each several
nation has its own special place for holding Divine service
according to its own rite, of whom the Latins have the
place where Christ appeared to Mary Magdalen in the
likeness of a gardener. Near the Church of the Holy
Sepulchre once dwelt the brethren of St. John of
Jerusalem, and their palace is now the common hospital
for pilgrims. This hospital is so great that one thousand
men can easily live therein, and can have everything that
they want there by paying for it. It is the custom in this
palace, or hospital, that every pilgrim should pay two

Venetian pennies[1] for the use of the hospital. If he sojourns therein for a year he pays no more, if he abides but for one day he pays no less. In my time there dwelt in this palace, or hospital, a matron named Margaret of Sicily, who had a brother a canon of the holy sepulchre, named Nicholas. This Margaret was of great use and service there, and to my certain knowledge suffered much misery and trouble for love of the Christians, and was always viewed by the Soldan with especial favour because of her usefulness.[2] You must know that canons of the holy sepulchre have great prerogatives and privileges, as I have read in their service-book, and they begin (the service for) all the hours of the day with *Alleluia*,[3] as we do when we say *In adjutorium*, etc., as though they were men to whom the whole world bore witness from afar. They read all the chief matters in the Gospel with gesticulation ; for instance, the deacon reads the Gospel on Easter Day as follows :[4] 'At that time Mary Magdalen, and Mary the mother of James, and Salome, brought spices, that they might come hither and anoint Jesus.' And when he comes to the words, ' He is not here, He is risen,' then the deacon points with his finger to Christ's sepulchre, and so in other cases. In front of the church, on the west side, there is the stone whereon Jesus rested awhile when bearing His cross, when His strength failed Him because of His tortures and the weight of the cross ; and there the Jews compelled Simon of Cyrene, who was coming from his village, to bear the cross. Near the church, a little way to the south, is the stone whereon Jesus stood when He said, ' Ye daughters of Jerusalem, weep not for Me, but for yourselves,' etc.

---

[1] Denarii. Fabri (i. 395) says 'two Venetian marks.'

[2] The ordinary text has *fidelitatem*. I prefer to read *utilitatem*, with the Berlin MS. marked ' B ' by Dr. F. Deycks.

[3] John of Wurzburg, chap. xii.

[4] Matt. xxvii. 56 ; Mark xv. 40 ; Luke xxiv. 1-10 ; John xix. 40. See ' Marino Sanuto,' III., vii. 2.

The pavement of the house of Pilate may be seen in
Jerusalem to this day; but it was then without the city,
and the house of Caiaphas, wherein they took counsel, and
he prophesied, saying, 'It is expedient that one man
should die for the people,' is three of the miles of that
country distant from Jerusalem. Moreover, in Jerusalem
there are to be seen very many other wonders and holy
places, about each one of which it would take long to tell
you. Going onward from Jerusalem, one comes to a city,
once fair, but now deserted, which stands in the hill country
of Judaea, and is called Zacharia. It is five miles distant
from Jerusalem. It was in this city that Zachariah and
Elizabeth, the parents of St. John the Baptist, dwelt, and
to it the Blessed Mary came from Nazareth after the
annunciation by the word of Gabriel, when Elizabeth met
her and the babe leaped in her womb, and the Blessed
Mary said, ' My soul doth magnify the Lord,' etc. On the
place where they met and embraced one another, an
exceeding fair church has been built, which is called
Magnificat to this day. This place is distant from
Nazareth three and a half days' journey of the short
journeys which our Lord's mother then made, as the
Gospel tells us,[1] 'Mary arose with haste and went into the
hill country of Judaea.' In this city also St. John the
Baptist was conceived and born. As one returns from this
city of Zacharia one sees the place where (the wood of)
Christ's cross is believed to have grown ;[2] moreover, by
the roadside one sees many tombs of the saints, hermitages, caves, and grottos, wherein to this day are found
many incorrupt and entire bodies of saints, whose names
God alone knows. As one comes back to Jerusalem this

---

[1] Luke i. 39.

[2] Wilhelm von Boldinsel (chap. viii) mentions this place, and says
that there was a fair church, and a convent of Georgian monks.

way, there is the place without the North Gate where the first martyr, St. Stephen, was stoned. Here a fair church seems to have stood, which now is overthrown, and it stands above the Valley of Jehoshaphat. In the Valley of Jehoshaphat there is a holy but not very beautiful church[1] built in honour of the Blessed Mary, into which one goes down sixty steps and comes to the Blessed Mary's sepulchre, which is adorned with more and better lamps and candles than Christ's sepulchre. The place where the sepulchre stands is not larger than what eight men can conveniently stand in, and the sepulchre of Christ and that of the Blessed Mary are both shaped alike. The place where this church stands was at the time of Christ's Passion the house of Annas, the Chief Priest, and it was there that Peter denied Christ. On the spot where he denied Him there stands a marble pillar for an everlasting memorial. It is believed that on the last day Christ will come to this valley as a strict Judge, and will reward every man according to his works. Through this same valley runs the brook Cedron, being the moisture and rain-water which comes from the hills on either side thereof. Near this brook, at the foot of the Mount of Olives, is the garden wherein Jesus was taken and was betrayed by Judas with a kiss. God when in the flesh often visited this garden with His disciples. A fair church stands at the place where Christ was taken, but nowadays the Saracens shut up their flocks and beasts to feed therein. A little way from the garden, to the left, beneath a rock, is the place where Christ prayed to the Father, saying, ' Father, if it be possible, let this cup pass from Me,' and in His fear He in His human weakness sweated blood. At the foot of

---

[1] ' Ecclesia devota sed non multum pulchra.'—Ludolph. ' Haec ecclesia non est pulchra, sed devota.'—W. von Boldinsel. The order in which these two writers describe the holy places agrees exactly.

the mountain opposite, whereon Jerusalem is built, are the bathing-pools of Siloam, and now there is a collection of putrid water. Over against the bathing-pool stands Absalom's statue, cunningly wrought, and of wondrous size.[1] Above the Valley of Jehoshaphat, to the south, is the potter's field, or Aceldama, also called the Field of Blood, which was bought with the price of blood to bury strangers in. But a certain Eastern history declares that only the worth of fifteen pennies was bought, which, indeed, may well be believed, because it does not take up the third part of the field.

XXXIX.—OF THE THIRTY PIECES OF SILVER.

We read in a history of those kings of the East who offered gifts to our Lord, that Terah, Abraham's father, made money, or pennies, at the bidding of a King of Mesopotamia named Ninus, and that he received thirty pieces of silver for his pay. These pieces of silver he gave to Abraham, who spent them during his wanderings in exile, and these same pieces of silver passed through divers hands until they came into the hands of the Ishmaelites, and with them Joseph was bought from his brethren. Afterwards, when Joseph bore rule in Egypt, these same pieces of silver came back into Joseph's hands from his brethren as the price of corn, and when they were restored to his brethren, his brethren gave them to Joseph's steward, who sent them to Sheba to buy merchandise for Pharaoh. Now, in Solomon's time, when the Queen of Sheba came from the East to hear his wisdom, she offered these thirty pieces of silver in the temple. In

---

[1] W. von Boldinsel mentions Siloam, but does not call the water putrid, and mentions Absalom's 'statue' in the same words as in the text, except that he says that it is *bonae magnitudinis*, whereas Ludolph says *mirae magnitudinis*.

the time of Rehoboam, when Nebuchadnezzar despoiled the temple and took away its treasure, he gave the thirty pieces of silver with other treasure to the King of Godolia, who was with him in his army, and so they remained with other treasures in the treasury of the Kings of Godolia until Christ's birth. At that time the kingdom of Godolia was removed to Nubia. Now, when our Lord was born, Melchior, the King of Nubia, saw in the star that Christ was born of a virgin. He therefore took the thirty pennies, because he could find no more noble or ancient gold in his treasury, and by God's will offered them to Christ. Afterwards the Blessed Virgin Mary, when fleeing into Egypt through fear of Herod, lost the thirty pennies, together with the rest of the presents of the Magi, at the place where the Garden of Balsam now is. A shepherd found them and kept them for thirty years. Then the fame of Jesus being noised abroad, this same shepherd came to Jerusalem, where Jesus healed his sickness. When Christ was preaching and teaching in the temple the shepherd offered Him the thirty pennies and the other presents of the Magi, but Jesus refused them, and bade him offer the pennies in the temple, and lay the other gifts upon the altar. The shepherd did so, and the Jews cast the thirty pennies into *corban*, and afterwards gave them to Judas for betraying Jesus.[1] Then when Judas brought them back again, they bought the potter's field for fifteen pennies, and gave the other fifteen to the

[1] John of Hildesheim, though his account is substantially the same, is somewhat more diffuse. For instance, at this point he explains that when the shepherd offered the gifts, the priest burned the frankincense on the altar, but put the gold and myrrh into the treasury. Probably John's was the 'long rambling story' alluded to by Fabri (i. 537). See *Quarterly Review*, October, 1846, art. 'Cologne Cathedral'; Theoderich, chap. xxxix., p. 59. Another version of the legend makes the thirty pieces to have been struck at Capernaum. See 'The Condition of Jerusalem,' in this series, part ii., p. 31.

soldiers who were guarding Christ's sepulchre; and when
that had been done with the pennies which had been pre-
destined, they straightway were divided and scattered
hither and thither. But until that was done which it was
fated should be done by them, they always kept together,
as you have heard. The Scripture calls them silver
pennies, because in old times they called all metal silver;[1]
but there is no doubt but what they were of gold. The
field of blood is not large,[2] as I have told you, but has an
exceeding deep pit dug in it, with a vaulted roof above it.
This vault is pierced with round holes, through which holes
dead bodies are cast into it, and after three days nothing
of them is found save bones. Were it not so, such a little
place would not be sufficient to contain so many dead
bodies. Near this field there is an exceeding pleasant
place with beauteous trees, which the preaching friars[3]
(Dominicans) were trying to buy when I was leaving; but
I know not whether they got it. Near it also there are
very many hermitages of saints, cells, and oratories full of
grace, which now are deserted. Likewise near it is the
cave wherein Peter hid himself after he had denied Christ,
and wept bitterly. Not far from this cave is the place
where Judas hanged himself in despair.

XL.—THE MOUNT OF OLIVES.

Near Jerusalem, toward the east, is the Mount of Olives,
which now is called the Mount of Lights, a very pleasant
place, with only the Valley of Jehoshaphat between it and
Jerusalem. The Mount of Olives is so much higher than
the city, that all within the city can be seen from its top,
and it is called the Mount of Olives because many olives

---

[1] John of Hildesheim tells this part in the same words.
[2] 'Vix ad semijactum lapidis,' says John of Hildesheim.
[3] Fabri, i. 535; ii. 380.

grow thereon; it is also called the Mount of Lights,[1] because by night the lights of the Lord's Temple shine over against it. The two eastern gates of Jerusalem leading to the mount are always shut, because the Valley of Jehoshaphat between the city and the mount is so steep that a man could scarce climb up and down on his hands and feet, and that one gate is now called the Golden Gate. On the Mount of Olives stands a fair church called St. Saviour's, on the place where forty days after His Passion Christ ascended meekly to His Father, and where the angels said that He should come again as a strict Judge. The mark of Christ's footsteps may be seen on the pavement of that church even to this day, and we read that when the Christians were first building and paving that church, whenever they came to the place where Christ's footprints were, and laid stones thereon, the stones always sprung off again even as a man would step, and so the footprints have remained to the present day. The church is open, for the vault could never by any means be made over the place through which Christ passed. On the Mount of Olives there also stands another chapel on the place where Christ said the Lord's Prayer and taught it to His disciples, and that chapel is still called Paternoster. Once also upon this mount there stood another chapel, now overthrown, at the place where Jesus saw the city and wept over it. On this same mount there is a small village[2] named Galilee, often mentioned in Scripture, wherein the disciples dwelt together. This is that Galilee whereof we read, ' Go into Galilee; there will you see Him, as He said to you'; and again, ' I will go before you into Galilee' (Matt. xxvi. 32). But there is another Galilee, which is a great land, and is three days' journey distant, as you shall be told hereafter. On this mount also there

---

[1] Fabri, i. 495.   [2] This must be the tower called 'Viri Galilei.'

were many dwellings of saints, and hermitages, and gracious oratories. Near the Mount of Olives is Bethphage, where on Palm Sunday Christ mounted the ass to ride into Jerusalem. A good rider He must have been, otherwise one never could tell that a man on an ass could have ridden down such a road, for this road comes down very steep and narrow from the Mount of Olives. A short half-mile from Bethany is Bethphage, once a very fair castle standing on the hillside. In it are three churches, whereof one stands on the place where Lazarus was raised from the dead, and his sepulchre is still to be seen there. The sepulchres of Christ, of the Blessed Mary, and of Lazarus are all shaped alike. The second church stands in the place where once was the house of Simon the leper, where Christ was asked to dinner, and the blessed Mary Magdalen came and anointed the head and the feet of Jesus, washed them with her tears, and wiped them with her hair, as the Scripture bears witness. The third church is made out of Martha's palace, wherein God in our weakness, when hungry and thirsty, naked and weary, was often received as a guest by Martha, refreshed, and entertained when homeless.

The Saracens who dwell there now shut up their oxen and beasts of burden in these churches. In this place Solomon set up his idol Moloch.[1]

XLI.—THE DESERT ; JERICHO ; SODOM AND GOMORRHA.

From Bethany one reaches the Jordan in one day, crossing a little wilderness called Montost.[2] In this wilder-

---

[1] 1 Kings xi. 7.

[2] I do not understand this word. Wilhelm von Boldinsel says (chap. viii.) : ' De hoc loco [Bethany] parva diaeta est in Jordanem, deserto quodam montoso medio existente,' etc. John of Hildesheim

ness St. John the Baptist taught, and ate locusts and wild honey in the same. In this wilderness also a certain man fell among thieves as he was going down from Jerusalem to Jericho, as the Scripture tells us. At the end of this wilderness is the mount which is called Quarentana, whereon Jesus fasted for forty days and forty nights, and was an hungered, and here the devil tempted Him to make bread of stones. Halfway up the mount a fair hermitage has been hewn out of the rock wherein Christ fasted, and wherein Georgian monks now dwell. In my time the King of Gazara[1] caused the road to be broken, so that the monks could not get down nor pilgrims get up, but when the Soldan heard of this he had the road well repaired, and granted leave to the monks to dwell there for ever. On the top of this mount stands a fair church in the place where Jesus was tempted of the devil. It is of this wilderness that we read, 'Jesus was led up of the Spirit into the wilderness to be tempted of the devil.'[2] Near this mount, toward the plain of Jordan, there is a fountain and an exceeding fair orchard, where Abraham dwelt when he came from Chaldaea, and built an altar there and called upon the name of the Lord. This place is called Abraham's Garden[3] to this day. After passing these places one comes into Jericho, once a royal and famous city, now brought down to a small village, but standing in an exceeding beauteous and fertile spot in the Valley of the Jordan. This is the Jericho[4] whose walls God cast down by a miracle, and gave it to Joshua, with a curse on him who should rebuild it. To this Jericho belonged

---

says (chap. xlii.) : 'Et inter Jordanum et Jerusalem est quedam pars deserti que ibidem Mentost vocatur, et in ipso deserto Johannes Baptista habitavit et penitenciam predicavit,' etc. Al. Montoft, Moncost.

[1] Fabri (ii. 56) copies this story ; but in his day the place was deserted.

[2] Matt. iv. 1.   [3] Theoderich, chap. xxviii.   [4] Josh. vi. 26.

Rahab the harlot and Zacchaeus[1] who was little of stature. It was the boys of this Jericho who mocked Elisha[2] the prophet, saying, 'Go up, thou bald head! go up, thou bald head!' and were devoured by two bears to avenge him, to all of which things the Scripture bears witness. Near Jericho is the place where Jesus lightened the eyes of the blind man as He passed by. Near Jericho there runs the brook which the prophet Elisha[3] made sweet, which before was bitter. Three short miles from Jericho is the Dead Sea, which is about eighty miles of this country long, where stood the great cities of Sodom and Gomorrha, Seboim and Adana, and all the places within them and near them, all of which cities, villages, castles, and fortresses God overwhelmed because of their detestable sins. No creature can use the water of this sea for any purpose whatever, and it has a most unbearable and evil stench, wherefore when the wind blows it poisons all the country round about. In storms it casts up many beauteous pebbles, but if anyone picks them up his hand will stink for three days so foully that he will not be able to bear himself. Some say that a man cannot sink therein. Of this I know nothing save what has been told me, and perchance no one has ever tried it. But I have heard from the people of those parts that in some parts of the sea one can find the bottom, and in some not. But as for the buildings which stood there before the great destruction, no traces of them can be seen ; indeed, a man can scarce approach it because of its vile and intolerable stench. Yet all the country round about is full of trees and great fruits,[4] exceeding fair to see ; but when these

---

[1] Luke xix. 3.   [2] 2 Kings ii. 23. It was not at Jericho, but at Bethel.
[3] 2 Kings ii. 20.

[4] Dead Sea fruit. Tac., 'Hist.,' v. 7 ; Josephus, 'De Bell. Jud.,' iv. 8 ; August., 'De Civ. Dei,' book xxi., chap. v. Compare Robinson's 'Palestine,' vol. ii., p. 472.

fruits are plucked and broken open, they are full of dust and ashes within, and for three days the hands of him who plucked them cannot be rid of a vile stench; for even all the country round about it is full of God's curse. In this country the serpent called *tyrus* is found and taken, whence what is called tyriac (treacle)[1] gets its name, for it is chiefly made thereof. This is a serpent not half an ell long, as thick as a man's finger, of a yellow colour mixed with red, and it is blind. No cure for its poison is known except cutting off the bitten limb. When it is angry it puts out its tongue like a flame of fire, and one would think that it was fire indeed, save that it does not burn the creature; it sets up the hair on its face like an angry boar, and its head at such times grows bigger. Were it not blind, I believe that no man could escape from it, for I have heard from those whose trade it is to catch these serpents, that if they bit a man's horse, they would kill the rider.[2] Near the Dead Sea, on the right hand toward the mountains of Israel, on a little hill, stands Lot's wife, turned into a pillar of salt. At this place in my time there were Templars, who had been made prisoners at the fall of Acre, who sawed wood here and there in the mountains for the Soldan's service, and did not know that the

---

[1] Θηριακή. Cf. Fabri, i. 537. See 'Carpentier's Glossary,' arts. *Thiriaca* and *Triaculum*. Littré gives the etymology of 'thériaque': 'Génev. *thériacle;* Provenç. *tiriaca, triacla;* Catal. *triaga;* Espagn. *teriaca, triaca;* Ital. *teriaca;* du Lat. *theriaca*, qui vient du Grec Θηριακή, sous-entendu ἀντίδοτος.' Under Θηριακή Liddell and Scott quotes Alexander of Tralles, v., p. 244, Galen, and Nicander's po-m on such antidotes. Under the word 'Treacle,' Bailey's Dictionary gives '[*triacle*, Fr., *triakel*, Du., *theriaca*, L., Θηριακή, Gr., of θήριον, Gr., a viper], a physical Composition made of Vipers and other Ingredients.' See Vincent of Beauvais's 'Speculum Naturale,' book xx., chap. xlvi.

[2] The story is to be found in John of Hildesheim, chap. xlii., as are also the stories about the Dead Sea fruit, 'Jor,' and 'Dan,' and St. John's arm at the monastery by the Jordan.

Order of the Templars had been suppressed ;[1] for they worked here and there in the mountains, and had seen no man from this side of the sea since they had been taken prisoners.   These men strongly dissuaded us from riding further along the shore of the Dead Sea, if we did not wish to lose our lives through its stench ; but they showed us the statue of Lot's wife, which we could see plainly a long way off.   Within the year the Soldan set these men free, together with their wives and children, in answer to some-one's intreaties, and they came to the Court of our Lord (the Pope), and were sent with honour to their homes ; one of them was a Burgundian, the other came from Thou-louse.   Not far from the statue of Lot's wife stood the city of Zoar, which by Lot's prayer was saved from destruction.   Beyond the Dead Sea toward the east, is the strongest castle[2] in the world, which in Arabic is called Arab ; in Chaldee, Schobach ; and in Latin, Montreal. It is said that there is no castle in the world to compare therewith, and it is girt about with three walls.   Within the first wall there is an exceeding lofty rock with three springs running out of it, which water all the land round about.   Within the second wall there grows enough corn to easily support all the people of the castle from one year to another.   Within the third wall there used to grow as much wine, but the vines have been grubbed up.   The whole world cannot take these things, except the trees and vines, away from the castle.   This castle once belonged to

---

[1] In 1307 the Grand Master and all the Knights Templars in Paris were arrested by order of Philip IV. (le Bel).   Their trial dragged on for five years, at the end of which the Order was abolished.

[2] The castle called Montreal or Petra by the Crusaders, was founded by Baldwin I. in 1115.   I suppose that this is the place mentioned by Fabri (ii. 402) under the name of 'the Mount Rama.'   The fortress of Kerak was on the east side of the Dead Sea, while Montreal stood at the south end of it.   Ludolph seems to have confused the two places.

the Christians, but their sins caused them most basely to lose it by their own treachery. The Soldan now always keeps his treasure in this castle, and his son and heir, and to this castle he always flees for refuge in time of need. At the foot of this castle is a village called Sabab, wherein dwell more than six thousand Christians, earnestly looking for the Redeemer of the Holy Land.

XLII.—OF THE RIVER JORDAN.

From the Dead Sea one comes to the Jordan, which is a river not ten paces wide. But albeit the Jordan is a small river, yet it is exceeding deep and muddy; it waxes and shrinks according to the season, and sometimes is so swollen with rain-water that it would float loaded ships. It has a very muddy bottom, sweet water, and excellent fish; it rises about four days' journey to the north of the Accursed Sea, at the foot of Mount Lebanon, from two streams called Jor and Dan. Passing through Galilee, it takes the names of both these rivers, and is called Jordan; but at the foot of Mount Carmel a brook runs out and falls into Jor. Near the Dead Sea, two short miles up the Jordan, is the place where Jesus was baptized by John; the place is called the Fords of the Jordan. Here Joshua and the children of Israel passed over dryshod. Here also the water of Jordan was divided at the bidding of Elijah the prophet, and here also the water was divided when Elisha struck it with Elijah's mantle. Near this place, not far from the bank of the Jordan, a fair monastery has been built in honour of John the Baptist, and is inhabited by Greek monks, who declare that they possess St. John's arm. This monastery has been removed a little way from the river bank because the waters sometimes overflow. All the Christians of the land, and even pilgrims from far-off lands, gather together at this place on the day of the Lord's Epiphany, and all read there in Latin the Gospel 'When Jesus was born in Bethlehem,'[1] etc., bless the water, and baptize the cross. All who have any sickness or disease then leap into the water, and most of them are healed of their infirmities in the sight of all men. In the Valley of the Jordan is the heap of foreskins,[2] the place of circumcision, the place of weeping, and the twelve stones which the children of Israel took out of the bed of the Jordan for a testimony. It was of these stones that John the Baptist spoke, when he said, 'The Lord[3] is able of these stones to raise up children unto Abraham.' This valley is called the Valley of Achan, because therein Achan was stoned because of the King's gold which he had stolen. It was in this valley also that Elijah was carried up to heaven in a chariot of fire. Not far—only two short miles away—from the place where Jesus was baptized, the Jordan enters the Dead or Accursed Sea, and is seen no more, and it is a question in the East why such blessed water should enter so accursed a place. Some say it is that the curse of the one may be allayed by the blessing of the other, others declare that it is swallowed up just at the entrance, both of which may well be believed; but to me it seems more likely that it is drunk up by the earth, for sometimes the rain-water running from all the hills round about makes the Jordan so great that it would not be possible for such a body of water to run into the sea without making it overflow, and flood all the country about it. The length of the river Jordan is, from its source to its end, about five-and-twenty of this country's miles. Beside the river Jordan there are very many monasteries of Greeks and schismatics, and hermitages full of grace. Every evening on the banks of this same river one may

[1] Matt. ii.
[2] Deut. xxvii. 2 ; Josh. iv. 3-20 ; v. 2.   [3] Matt. iii. 9.

see countless wild beasts, both great and small, drinking, especially lions, foxes, roes, stags, hares, wild boars, and the like, which walk among men like tame beasts. In my time[1] there used to be always a lion at one particular place, on the further bank of the Jordan, who would watch people passing by, wagging his tail like a dog, and did not run away, neither did he hurt anyone by day or by night. At last one of our archers,[2] wishing to frighten and anger him, shot an arrow at him. The lion did not stir, but seemed to pray towards the arrow ; but when the man shot another, the lion reared up at it, as though he would catch it with his mouth and paws. After this the lion was seen no more in this place, but did much hurt both to men and beasts of burden. Of other wild beasts there are so many here that the country people drive them to market like sheep. Not far from hence is the place called the hills[3] of Jordan, where the children of Reuben and the children of Gad and the half-tribe of Manasseh built 'a great altar to see to,' when they came into their possessions.

XLIII.—OF RAMATHA, SHILOH, EMMAUS, SICHAR, SAMARIA, AND GALILEE.

From the Jordan one comes in three days to Galilee, Judaea, and Samaria. After seeing many sights, one leaves Jerusalem on the left, and comes to the city of Ramatha,[4] once a fair city, and to this day tolerably well peopled, standing on Mount Ephraim. In this city dwells at this day the Cadi—that is, the Bishop of the Saracens—

---

[1] Fabri (ii. 27) tells this story, which he had clearly read in Ludolph. Compare Phocas, chap. xxiii., p. 28.

[2] *Quidam sagittarius noster.*

[3] A.V., 'the borders of Jordan ;' R.V., 'the region of Jordan' (Josh. xxii. 10).

[4] 'Ramathaim-Zophim, of Mount Ephraim' (1 Sam. i. 1 ; xxv. 1 ; xxviii. 3).

and here we once had much trouble about some Christians who had been taken prisoners there through their own folly, before we set them free. The prophet Samuel was born in this city, and buried in it. It was near this city that Habakkuk[1] the prophet was carrying the harvesters their dinner, when he was caught up by the angel and carried to Daniel in the lions' den at Babylon. Not far from Ramatha was a once fair, but now deserted, city named Arimathea, the birthplace of Joseph who buried Christ. Near this place, three miles off, once stood a famous city, which now is a small village, called Shiloh, where the Ark of the Covenant stood, and the Hebrews gathered together there to pray. Not far from Shiloh is Emmaus, once a fair city, but now deserted, where Jesus appeared to His disciples after His resurrection. This city is now called Nicopolis.[2] Near Nicopolis, on the right hand, once stood two very famous cities, now deserted—to wit, Gibeon and Ajalon[3]—where Joshua fought against five kings, and at his bidding the sun lengthened its course, until he overcame the enemies of Israel. Moreover, not far from Shiloh, in the country of Samaria, there once stood a fair city in a valley, which city was called Sichar, and is now called Neapolis, and at this day is all but deserted. It was here that Dinah,[4] Jacob's daughter, was ravished, and avenged by his sons. Near this road there once stood a fair little church, now much ruined, wherein is Jacob's Well,[5] beside which Christ, when sitting, weary with journeying in our human frailty, asked the woman of Samaria for water to

---

[1] See Abbot Daniel in this series, p. 49. Odoricus de Foro-Julii (ed. Laurent, 1864, p. 156) says: 'Extra muros Joppe est capella Abacuc prophetae, ubi angelus,' etc. See also Fabri, i. 543, note; Poloner, p. 31, note.

[2] A mistake. See Raumer's 'Palestine,' p. 169.

[3] Josh. x. 12.   [4] Gen. xxxiv. 25.   [5] John iv. 18.

refresh Him, and said to her, 'Thou hast had five husbands,' as the Scripture tells us. It was near this well that Jeroboam, King of Israel, made golden calves which the children of Israel worshipped. Also in a field near this place David slew Goliath, and very many other notable places are to be seen along this road, whereof it would take long to tell. Going on from Sichar, one comes to Samaria, which once was the capital of the whole country, wherefore all that land is called the country of Samaria. This was once an exceeding fair, famous, royal, and very great city, as its ruins bear witness, and in situation is in all respects very like the city of Jerusalem. The Kings of Israel once dwelt in this city. In this city also St. John the Baptist was buried between the prophets Elisha and Obadiah. This city, which of old was· called Samaria, was afterwards called Sebaste, and is now called Yblim,[1] from which the chief tribe of Christians in that land are called 'of Yblin' (*sic*) even to this day. They were at first French knights, and on the recovery of the Holy Land this city fell to their lot. When one has seen the aforesaid sights at Samaria, one goes on over the plains of Galilee, leaving the mountains behind. Galilee is a province of the Promised Land, and is a noble country, rich in plains, hills, pastures, grass, and other good things, with exceeding fruitful and pleasant valleys. On its plains and the slopes of its hills stand the following cities—to wit, Nain, Capernaum, Bethsaida, and Cana of Galilee; but all these are now deserted, or all but deserted, and they do not look as if they had ever been of much account. What things God in our flesh wrought therein is written at large in the Gospels, and therefore I do not care to repeat it. Near Nain is Mount Endor, at

[1] 'At the going up to Gur, which is by Ibleam' (2 Kings ix. 27). See Anon. VI., p. 58; and Fetellus, p. 32.

whose foot runs the brook Kishon. This land of Galilee
also has been illustrated and glorified by very many of
Christ's miracles. At the borders of Galilee are the mountains of Gilboa, which are low hills, greatly abounding
with green herbs, grass, and pasture. It was on these
hills that Saul and Jonathan and the children of Israel
fell, and of them David said, ' Ye mountains of Gilboa, let
there be no dew or rain upon you.'[1] Some say that no
dew or rain falls upon them, which is false, because one
can see that very many exceeding fair monasteries once
stood upon them, whose paintings show that they belonged to the order of the Cistercians, and to that of
St. Bene't. In the neighbourhood of the mountains of
Gilboa stood the city of Bethulia, wherein dwelt Judith,
who cut off the head of Holofernes hard by ; but the city
is now destroyed. After one has seen each of these
things, one leaves the plain of Galilee and comes to
Nazareth, which once was a famous city, and is a very fair
one to this day, standing in a flowery and beauteous vale,
girt about on all sides by mountains. It is not walled,
but its houses stand apart from one another ; yet it is well
peopled. In this city God deigned to announce through
Gabriel to the Blessed Virgin Mary that He was made
man. In this city there has been built a great and fair
church, wherein, near the choir, there is a beauteous chapel
on the spot where God announced that He was made man
for our sake, where also the Blessed Virgin conceived God
and man. In this chapel there is a small pillar, against
which Gabriel stood when he announced Christ, and his
figure remains imprinted on the column, like the figure of
a seal on wax, even to this day. Behind the church there
is a fountain from which the Blessed Virgin was ever wont
to draw water, and near which she very often was spoken

[1] 2 Sam. i. 21.

to and comforted by angels. In my time the Saracens had greatly blocked up this fountain out of spite against Christians and pilgrims, but they never were able to stop the flow of its water. The Saracens also desecrate this holy and glorious church in divers ways, for they skin dead animals, such as asses, camels, dogs, and oxen, therein, and cast their carcases therein, so that one can scarce visit these most holy places for the stench. There dwell in Nazareth most evil Saracens, wicked and noble, who are called Dehes; they take scarcely any heed of the Soldan, but to enter the city one needs their passport and safe-conduct beyond everything else. One mile from Nazareth there is a rock on a mountain, which is called the Lord's Leap, where Jesus passed through the midst of the Jews and went His way,[1] when they would have cast Him down it, as the Scripture and Gospel tell us. The figure of Jesus may be seen to this day imprinted as though on soft wax upon the rock through which He passed. Going on from this place, one comes at mid-day to Mount Tabor, which is a mount standing all by itself on a plain. It is very high, but not wide, and is in all ways very like the hill called Dezenberg,[2] in the diocese of Paderborn.

On the top of this mount Jesus Christ was transfigured, and His face shone like the sun, in the presence of Peter, John, and James, and there Moses and Elias appeared talking with Him. On the place where He was transfigured there once was built a noble and royal monas-

---

[1] 'Ueber die herrliche Lage des Desenberg's, verg. Fürstenberg, Monum. Paderborn, s. 165 ff.—F. Deycks.

[2] *Transiens per medium illorum ibat.* Luke iv. 30; John viii. 59; x. 39. See Wright's note to Sir John Maundeville, chap. x. 'Early Travels in Palestine,' Bohn's Series. The words appear on some English coins, *e.g.*, the 'Noble' of Henry V., and the 'Spur-Ryal' of Elizabeth.

tery of the Order of St. Bene't. Its Abbot used a leaden bulla, like the Pope. I have seen many of these bullae. You must know that in the lands beyond the sea the Feast of the Lord's Transfiguration is very solemnly kept ; it comes on the day of SS. Felix and Agapetus,[1] and is then celebrated with new wine. On that day all nobles and citizens specially meet together at church ; they place banners upon their churches, and watch with rejoicings all night long. The *Office* of the Mass is, *Dominus dixit ad me filius*, etc. *Dies sanctificatus illuxit*, etc. The Gospel is, *Assumpsit Jesus Petrum et Johannem*, etc. The top of this mount and the monastery has been occupied by the Saracens, for it was once well fenced with walls and towers. Now on the top it is all ruined and deserted ; but the walls and towers remain for the most part. About this mount one reads many other things, to which the Scripture bears witness. At the foot of Mount Tabor is an exceeding great and strong castle, named Blansagarda[2] (Blanche Garde), which was built by the Christians to defend the way up to the mount, for the mount was always held by the Saracens. In those parts there is a large and noble tribe of Christians, called ' of Blanche Garde,' for this was their castle ; but where their parents were born before the recovery of the Holy Land no man knows, and I have often been asked by them whether there were any people in my country who said that they had relations in those parts, or who bore their arms on their shields. From Mount Tabor one goes on to Mount Hermon, which is a fair and pleasant mount, and comes

---

[1] Properly SS. Felicissimus and Agapetus, August 6.

[2] A mistake. The castle of Blanche Garde was built by King Fulk I. in 1138 on Tell-es-Safieh, not far from Ascalon. It was also called Alba Specula. It was destroyed in 1191 by Saladin, and subsequently rebuilt. Compare Stanley's ' Sinai and Palestine,' chap. vi.

into the spacious plains of Galilee, where Sisera and his army fell. Thence one comes to the shores of the Sea of Galilee, to the city of Synareth,[1] which was afterwards called Tiberias, and is now called Tybaria. It stands by the sea-shore, and is a poor place, and never was much more ; but once it had a bishop for its noble lord, to whom the greater part of the Sea of Galilee belonged. Near this city there are natural hot baths, like those at Aachen in this country. It seems that on the shores of the Sea of Galilee there used to stand many other cities and villages, though none of much account, wherein Christ's disciples and other poor men and fishermen dwelt, and dwell to this day. The Sea of Galilee or of Tiberias measures twenty miles of this country in circuit, and hath abundance of sweet-tasted and excellent fishes, and exceeding sweet water. The river Jor runs into this sea on one side, and the river Dan on the other ;[2] they may be seen passing through the sea, and they come out of it in one stream, which then is called the Jordan. Upon and near this sea, God in the likeness of man wrought many miracles. It was from this sea that Jesus called Peter and Andrew, and made them Apostles. It was upon this sea that Christ walked dry-shod, and caught Peter when he was beginning to sink. It was on this sea that Jesus slept in the ship and stilled the wind when the storm arose. Upon this sea Jesus when in our mortal frailty often sailed, and illustrated it with many miracles. It was beside this sea that Jesus appeared to His disciples after His resurrection, and ate the broiled fish and honeycomb. At this place there once stood a fair church, which now is destroyed. Near this sea there is a mount. At its foot God fed five thousand

---

[1] Num. xxxiv. 11 ; Luke v. 1.

[2] 'This is a mistake, or a confusion of this sea with Lake Merom.'— F. Deycks.

people with five loaves and two fishes, as the Gospel bears witness. On the top of this mount, on the north side, there is a lofty and exceeding strong castle, which, together with its village, is called Japhet,[1] wherein in my time a Jew from Westphalia dwelt with his wife. Not far from this castle there once stood a fair city named Dan, but it is now almost deserted. This is the other end of the Promised Land, for the Promised Land reaches from Dan to Beersheba from north to south, and is about twenty-five miles long, and in width from Jericho to Joppa, from east to west, it is about eleven miles of this country, as I have heard from the Soldan's couriers, and from exceeding trustworthy people of the country, who also described the land. Not far from Dan, toward the north, is the once fair city of Bolynas,[2] now called Caesarea Philippi, pleasantly situated at the foot of Mount Lebanon, but scantily peopled. It was near it that Jesus asked His disciples, 'Whom do men say the Son of man is?' as the Gospel testifies.[3] Not far from this city there is a spring near the mountain, which divides Idumaea from Phoenicia ; this spring is commonly called Sabbath, because it does not flow on Saturdays. After you have seen all these sights, you cross the Jordan at the place where it first leaves Galilee. In this land beyond Jordan two tribes and a half-tribe received their inheritance. Here also the Jordan divides Galilee from Idumaea, and one goes on and sees many villages and places not mentioned in Scripture, and comes, if one chooses, to a village where Job is buried. It was near this village that St. Paul was cast down and converted, and it stands about one day's journey distant from Damascus.

---

[1] Japhia, fortified by Josephus, taken by Vespasian.
[2] Belinas, the ancient Paneas.   [3] Matt. xvi. 13.

XLIV.—THE CITY OF DAMASCUS.

Going on from this village, one comes to Damascus. Damascus is an exceeding ancient city, founded by Damascus, Abraham's servant. It stands on the place where Cain killed his brother Abel, and is an exceeding noble, glorious, and beauteous city, rich in all manner of merchandise, and everywhere delightful, but more by artificial than by natural loveliness, abounding in foods, spices, precious stones, silk, pearls, cloth-of-gold, perfumes from India, Tartary, Egypt, Syria, and places on our side of the Mediterranean, and in all precious things that the heart of man can conceive. It is begirt with gardens and orchards, is watered both within and without by waters, rivers, brooks, and fountains, cunningly arranged, to minister to men's luxury, and is incredibly populous, being inhabited by divers trades of most cunning and noble workmen, mechanics, and merchants, while within the walls it is adorned beyond belief by baths, by birds that sing all the year round, and by pleasures, refreshments, and amusements of all kinds. Each trade dwells by itself in a particular street, and each workman, according to his craft and his power, makes in front of his house a wondrous show of his work, as cunningly, nobly, and peculiarly wrought as he can, outdoing his neighbours if possible, so that he adorns and decorates his house more beautifully than I can tell you. The merchants do likewise with their merchandise, and all handicrafts are wrought there wondrously well and with exceeding great skill. But they sell everything very dear. Rich citizens have all kinds of singing-birds and birdlets hanging in front of their houses, such as nightingales, quails, larks, francolins, and the like, and they sing wondrously and equally well all the year round, but better in winter time

than in the summer heat; and you may hear all other
kinds of birds, such as crows, pies, hoopoes, blackbirds,
and the like, who can be taught human speech, talking
like men in divers tongues. Though the city is so full of
people, and though all the merchandise is left almost
unguarded, yet there is no man so old that he can remember anyone ever to have been slain there, and it is
very seldom that any of the goods for sale are stolen.
Each sort of thing that is sold there has a special market
to itself. In the market where victuals are sold there may
be seen every day the greatest crowd of people ever seen
together in one place, and every kind of food that you can
think of may be found there most exquisitely cooked.
They take the greatest care with these things, and sell
them all by weight and scales ; also sundry different sorts
of bread are sold there. In Damascus there is an exceeding strong castle belonging to the Soldan, in which the
King of Damascus dwells. In the year of our Lord one
thousand three hundred and forty-one, on St. George's
Eve, there was a persecution and murder of Christians
by the King and mob of Damascus, even as of late[1] there
was of the Jews in this country ; but the persecution did
not last for more than a month, and by God's grace was
well avenged through the Soldan, as you will hear hereafter. In Damascus there are very many churches, both
of Catholics and of heretics, and monasteries full of grace.
Of these the Saracens have taken one fair church to be
a church for themselves, wherein rests the body of that
most learned doctor and weighty authority, St. John of
Damascus. On the front of this church God's majesty
still remains nobly painted. Moreover, the river Pharphar
is artificially made to flow through Damascus, and turns

---

[1] According to Dr. F. Deycks there was a *Juden verfolgung* in
Germany in 1348-9.

many cunningly-devised mills. Round about Damascus there are endless orchards and gardens, which bear grass, herbs, fruit, roses, and flowers all the year round, and are charming because of the songs of all kinds of birds and birdlets, who sing more in the winter time than in the summer heat. These gardens and orchards surround the city for a distance of about two miles, and the whole country, and even far-off lands, abound with their fresh fruit all the year round, wherefore in the East it is a common saying, ' Damascus is the head of Syria,' and the Greeks, out of their love and respect for it, always call their eldest sons Polydamas—that is, City of Damascus.[1] It would take long to tell of the other wonders and beauties of Damascus. From Damascus it is less than one day's journey to the mount which God showed to Abraham, that he should sacrifice his son Isaac thereon. This mount is called Seyr, or Sardenay.[2] One first crosses

[1] Dr. F. Deycks thinks this another proof that Ludolph did not understand Greek.

[2] ' *De Damasco processi ad imaginem beate Virginis in Sardanii, ubi est locus fortis super petram ad modum castelli, muratus in circuitu, in quo satis pulchra est ecclesia. Retro majus altare in muro tabula quaedam tota nigra et humida cernitur, in qua imago gloriosae Virginis olim depicta fuisse asseritur; sed propter vetustatem nihil de lineamentis figurae cernitur in eadem, nisi quod in aliqua parte color rubeus mihi videbatur aliqualiter apparere. Haec tabula mediocris quantitate est, supra vas quoddam marmoreum posita intra murum cancellis ferreis premunita. De ipsa visibiliter oleum quasi continue stillat, quod monachi recipientes de vase marmoreo quod subtus est, per cancellos immisso cochleari peregrinis distribuunt satis large. Per omnem modum videtur esse oleum olivae. Dicitur quod pro certo aliquando de hac imagine oleum miraculose fluxerit; sed si hoc quod modo fluit divino fluit miraculo, rationaliter dubito, et etiam multi alii de veritate hujus facti non immerito alternantur. Monachi et moniales in predicto claustro sunt degentes. In casali pulchro quod sub monte est, Christiani schismatici commorantur, bono vino sati abundantes. Hic locus a Damasco sejungitur ad mediam diuturnam.*' —Wilhelm von Boldinsel. See also Sir John Maundeville, chap. xi. ; Fabri, i., p. 391.

the two rivers of Damascus, Abana and Pharphar. Upon
this rocky mount Seyr, or Sardenay, a fair monastery has
been built in honour of St. Mary ; it is built on the rock
in an exceeding strong place, fenced about on every side
with exceeding strong walls like a castle, and is inhabited
by Greek monks and nuns. In this monastery, on the
spot where Abraham would have sacrificed Isaac, there
stands a fair church, wherein, behind the altar, in a semi-
circular arch in the wall, there is a figure of the Blessed
Mary suckling her child, painted from the waist upwards
upon a wooden tablet, and fenced with iron bars ; but the
painting is so black with age and kisses that one can
scarce make out that it was a figure, beyond that a little
red colour can still be seen in the clothing. Nevertheless,
through this figure God hath wrought many blessings,
wonders, and acts of grace. We read that in the times
when the Christians held the Holy Land in possession, a
certain widow, wishing to serve God, chose for herself and
made a hermitage on this mount, which she wished no man
to know of, that her devotions might not be hindered by
any worldly business. Howbeit she had one matron in
her secret, who from time to time visited her, brought her
necessaries, and ministered to her. It befell that once this
matron, her confidant, was about to visit Jerusalem and
the other holy places. The widow hermit humbly and
devoutly begged her that she would bring her a picture of
the Blessed Mary painted on a tablet, because from the
bottom of her heart she earnestly longed for it. The
matron promised to do this, and being given leave by the
hermit widow, went tc holy Jerusalem, and, after visiting
all the holy places, obtained a tablet with a picture of
St. Mary, and journeyed to this Mount Seyr, or Sardenay.
When she was near the Jordan a terrible lion attacked her.
She could not flee, but with her hand protected herself

against the lion's spring with the tablet, as with a shield.
The lion as soon as he touched the tablet burst asunder,
and the matron continued her interrupted journey, and
reached the mountain, but she hid what had befallen her
from the hermit widow. She told her many other things
about the holy places, and after she had told her all, the
widow asked the matron whether she had brought her the
tablet with the figure painted thereon. The matron, who
thought that the picture would always have the same
virtues which it had before, said that she had not brought
it, but that she had forgotten it. When the widow heard
this, she was sorry and deeply grieved, and could not help
bursting into tears. But at last, when the matron would
have gone her way, all the doors of the hermitage and
chapel closed and firmly shut her in. Seeing that this was
done by the will of God, the matron presently confessed
to the widow that she had the tablet, and told her throughout what had befallen her on her journey with regard to the
lion, and other matters. When the widow heard this, she
many times gave thanks to God, received the tablet with
joy, respect, and devotion, and put it in the place where it
now stands. With tears and prayers, she gave honour to
Christ for the picture. At length this picture plainly
sweated oil, and the oil ran down into a little hollow made
in front of the picture, and does run into it to this day;
but because of the number of pilgrims, the monks now
eke it out with other oil and give it to pilgrims. But there
is no doubt that the picture does sweat oil, and within a
year this oil changes into milk, and the milk afterwards
changes into blood, which I have often seen with my
own eyes. Often at different times I have seen the oil
thus changed, and I have often had some of the oil thus
miraculously changed. This oil has great virtue against
storms at sea; when it is hung up in a bottle in the ship's

stern, the fiercest tempest straightway is still, which thing
I have often clearly seen. In many ways it is plain that
God hath an especial love for this place or mount, which
He showed to Abraham that he might sacrifice his son
thereon, because He hath wrought such miracles in honour
of His mother Mary, whose image is there painted, and
that even after so many troubles and invasions of the land
have come to pass, and the land itself has been so many
times and so strangely lost and won by divers peoples,
yet the monks and nuns of this place have ever remained
unharmed. We read, and the thing is still fresh in men's
minds, that when Haloon, who took Baldach, of whom I
have already made mention, had ravaged Egypt and all
Syria and the whole country, the monks and nuns of
this place were afraid, and thought of leaving it. Here-
upon God and the Blessed Virgin visibly appeared to
them and comforted them, so that they had no more fear
at all, and did not leave the place; for they wished to
remain near God and the Virgin, who in visible shape
encouraged them all, and they never thereafter received
any hurt or damage from either man or beast, but in my
time were always in especial grace and favour with the
Soldan, who did them much good, and in everything protected them like a father. At the foot of the Mount Seyr
there is a very great and fair village, wherein dwell Greeks
and Syrians. It abounds with good wine and very many
other good things, and there both in summer and in
winter, year after year, bunches of fresh grapes are found
on the vines, which, indeed, are specially guarded and set
apart for this purpose; and many other wonders and
miracles hath God wrought upon this mount, out of His
singular affection for it, by means of that picture, whereof
it would take long to tell.

XLV.—Of the Vale of Bokar, Lebanon, and Beyrout.

Journeying onward from Mount Seyr, one sees many things which need not be mentioned on the way, and leaving the afore-mentioned cities of Arimathea and Tripoli on the right hand, one comes to a valley named Bokar, which to this day is called the Plain of Noah, for there Noah dwelt after the flood. This plain is exceeding fertile and rich, abounding greatly in meadows, pastures, trees, fountains, flocks, fishes, and corn; it is shut in between mountains, and is inhabited by Saracen husbandmen. When you have seen and passed by all this, you come to Mount Lebanon, whereof also I have already made mention, and to the Black Mountains, which reach as far as Antioch, and whereon grows the wood of which the bows of crossbows[1] are made. This wood is carried away from these mountains to distant lands and countries. At the foot of this mountain dwells a vast multitude of Christians conforming to the Latin rite and the Church of Rome, many of whose bishops I have seen consecrated by Latin archbishops, and who ever long with singular eagerness for the coming of Crusaders and the recovery of the Holy Land.

After having seen all these and many other admirable villages, places, and hamlets, one comes into a city by the sea called Beyrout, whereof I have already made mention. This city is a common thoroughfare for pilgrims, and near it the glorious martyr St. George slew the dragon, and converted the city and all the country to the Christian faith. From Beyrout a man can return to any country

---

[1] Marino Sanuto (lib. ii., pars iv., chap. xxii.) says that the best wood for this purpose grew in Corsica.

he pleases on this side of the Mediterranean Sea, a matter which I leave to his own choice to settle.

These are the journeyings in the Holy Land, which are trustworthy, although not along the common pilgrim-routes, wherein I have viewed at my leisure all the aforesaid holy places and oratories, in the state and form wherein they appeared in the aforesaid years of our Lord.

And I know that in no respect can my account be impugned by any man living, for I bear testimony of what I have seen or have heard from truthful men. This account I have, as is most justly due, written out of the devotion and respect which I owe to the Right Reverend Father and Lord in Christ, Lord Baldwin, Bishop of the Church of Paderborn, and in the name of the Lord I have begun and finished the same, to whom be praise and glory for ever and ever. Amen.

INDEX.

THE END.

BILLING AND SONS, PRINTERS, GUILDFORD.

Printed by Printforce, United Kingdom